SEWING WITH AFRICAN WAX PRINT FABRIC

SEWING WITH AFRICAN WAX PRINT FABRIC

25 VIBRANT PROJECTS FOR HANDMADE CLOTHES AND ACCESSORIES

ADAKU PARKER

CICO BOOKS

LONDON NEW YORK

This book is dedicated to my children.

Published in 2021 by CICO Books
An imprint of Ryland Peters & Small Ltd
20–21 Jockey's Fields, London WC1R 4BW
341 E 116th St, New York, NY 10029

www.rylandpeters.com

10 9 8 7 6 5 4 3 2 1

Text © Adaku Parker 2021
Design, illustration, and photography
© CICO Books 2021

A CIP catalog record for this book is available from the Library of Congress and the British Library.

ISBN: 978-1-78249-877-3

Printed in China

Editor: Katie Hardwicke
Photographers: James Gardiner, Julian Ward
Stylist: Nel Haynes
Illustrators: Cathy Brear and Stephen Dew

In-house editor: Martha Gavin
Art director: Sally Powell
Head of production: Patricia Harrington
Publishing manager: Penny Craig
Publisher: Cindy Richards

CONTENTS

INTRODUCTION TO AFRICAN WAX PRINT FABRIC

ORIGINS

"African wax print" describes cotton fabrics that are printed using the industrial wax-resist method. These bold and often brightly-colored textiles feature a range of traditional and contemporary African motifs. The fabrics have an interesting and complex cultural history, and as a result you might hear them being called African Wax Print, Dutch Wax Print, or Ankara Hollandaise.

Cotton has been woven in Africa since the sixth century AD, and would have been printed using natural dyes. However it was the Dutch that introduced industrially wax-printed cotton designs to the African continent during the early to mid-nineteenth century. At that time, the Netherlands ruled what was then called Dutch East India (present-day Indonesia) and Dutch textile merchants created what we now know as African Wax print by imitating the Indonesian Batik print. The traditional Batik method involves hand-painting intricate designs onto cloth using beeswax. Colors are then added to the design and the waxed areas "resist" the penetration of the dye. When the wax is removed, the patterns are revealed.

The Dutch sought to mechanize this process, with a view to mass producing these fabrics and selling them to the Indonesians. Their modernized method involved transferring the design to cylindrical plates (copper rollers) that were covered in wax. These plates then transfered the pattern to both sides of the fabric. This created areas of the fabric, covered in wax, that would "resist" the color penetration. The fabric was then plunged into a vat of indigo dye and the non-waxed areas became bright blue. After some of the wax had been removed, and the fabrics had dried, colors were added one after the other using a stamp or block. It is generally very difficult to produce fabrics that are printed on both sides with the same pattern and color, so this unique characteristic is something that African wax print manufacturers aspire to achieve and are celebrated for.

The Indonesians, however, were unimpressed with the brighter, graphic wax prints that the Dutch had produced, as the mechanized dyeing process caused a veined or crackling effect that they saw as imperfections. At this time, some 700 soldiers from the Gold Coast in modern day Ghana had returned home from fighting in Java, bringing with them the new fabrics. What the Indonesians had seen as flaws, West Africans considered to be a testament to the quality of the printing process. And so, African wax printing begins in Africa.

PATTERNS AND MEANINGS

For nearly a century, African wax print fabrics contained many Indonesian designs. It wasn't until the early twentieth century that some textile designers began looking to the African continent itself for inspiration, where the motifs are often imbued with social, historical, or cultural meanings.

RIPPLE EFFECT

Also known as "nsubra," meaning waterwell, the circular repeat on this beautiful fabric is supposed to represent a stone being thrown into a well, causing a ripple effect. It is a very popular print and has been reproduced in numerous designs and colorways.

IRONS

The fabric used for the Christie Circle Skirt on page 28, has different-colored electric irons repeated throughout the design, in a nod to a time when these were a new modern convenience, owned by the middle classes in West Africa. At this time, the fabric would have been worn as a status symbol. Other appliances signifying status used as motifs include cell phones, washing machines, and computers.

CANDELABRA AND LIGHTBULBS

This fabric, used in the Etta sleeveless shirt dress on page 54, features spectacular alternating candelabra and lightbulbs, beaming out rays of light. The fabric dates back to the 1950s and would have reflected the wealth of its wearer—a candelabra would have had pride of place in only the wealthiest homes.

ANIMALS

From horses, chickens, and peacocks to turtles, crocodiles, and butterflies, animals are a recurring theme in African wax print fabrics. The use of animals has some historical connection with Adinkra symbols (see below.) The Penny Coin Purse, on page 74, features a mythical winged creature.

ADINKRA

Some fabrics may feature ancient symbols, known as Adinkra, that represent concepts or sayings. The historical roots of these symbols date back to the times of the Akan people of Ghana, West Africa. They are believed to have their origin from Gyaman, a former kingdom on the Ivory Coast, and to have migrated from the Sahara in the eleventh century.

WORKING WITH AFRICAN WAX PRINT FABRIC

PREPARING YOUR FABRIC

When working with African wax print fabrics, either for dressmaking, bag making, patchwork, quilting, or upholstery, treat them as you would any medium-weight cotton. The fabric has a stiff, waxy feel to it and will need to be prepared before sewing.

African wax print fabrics come in bolts of either 6 or 12 yards (5.5 or 11 meters), with the manufacturers' stickers or labels on the "right" side of the fabric at one end. These labels can be removed using a steam iron. Place the iron onto the "wrong" side of the fabric and use the steam to soften the industrial glue used to attach the labels. Do this carefully so as not to tear the label and once the glue is soft, the labels will easily peel away. Do this before you wash the fabric.

To soften the fabric, pre-wash it on a cool (86°F/30°C) wash. When dry, press using the medium steam setting on your iron.

African wax fabric is printed on both sides, so there is little difference between the "right side" and the "wrong side" of the fabric. In order to tell one from the other, you may use the selvage, which is printed with the manufacturer's details and quality statements. On the "right" side, this writing is clearly legible. However, on the "wrong" side, this writing is not decipherable. Before cutting into your fabric, mark the "wrong" side so that you can tell it apart from the "right" side once some or all of the selvage has been cut away. You can either use chalk to mark the wrong side, or use a pin with the head visible on the right side of the fabric.

PATTERN MATCHING

Follow these tips when choosing and pattern matching your fabric in order to showcase as much of the African wax print design as possible. See also page 109 for pattern-matching techniques.

• Small-scale prints are ideal for garment patterns with multiple smaller pieces, such as shirts, where pattern matching is not as straightforward.

• Choose large-scale prints for garment patterns with only a few larger pieces, such as a shift dress or a skirt, as cutting into the design multiple times will diminish the impact of a spectacular motif.

• Take care with placement of circular motifs in dressmaking; avoid the apex of the bust. If you do use a circular design for tops, you can insert panels into the pattern to break up the design.

• For directional designs, those that point in one direction (downward when held one way, upward when turned 180 degrees), cut either on the cross grain or straight grain, depending on the most flattering finish.

• Take care that your prints follow the same direction through the garment, such as all pointing downward in bodice, skirt, and sleeves (unless this is a considered part of your design!).

• With non-directional prints, find the most economical way of cutting out by placing the pattern pieces as close together as possible.

• With large motifs, such as a flower, ensure that the placement of the motif on the front panel is mirrored on the back panel.

• When working with larger motifs that require pattern matching, allow extra fabric when purchasing, for example if the pattern suggests 3yd (2.7m) for your size, buy 4yd (3.6m) minimum.

• Look for the repeat in the fabric and match that repeat (i.e. the mirror image) so that when you cut out a skirt front and back, for example, the front and the back are identical.

• Some African wax prints are printed by hand using block or stamp printing methods and the repeats across the fabric

are not always exact. This makes it difficult (although not impossible) to measure a repeat and to pattern match precisely at seams. Instead, why not try to pattern match on the front or back bodice with the motif centered or off-center, with the entirety of the motif contained in one pattern piece or panel.

• For pants, jumpsuits, and culottes, match the outer side seam where possible.

• As with all fabrics, cut on the bias when the fabric will be sitting against the neckline, armhole, or wrist. To find the bias, fold one corner of the fabric over until the side that is at right angles to the selvage is lined up with the selvage. The resulting fold line is the bias at 45 degrees to the selvage.

ALTHEA A-LINE SKIRT

SIZES
US 4–22 (UK 8–26/EU 36–54)

FINISHED MEASUREMENTS
Length: 30in (76cm)

MATERIALS
Sizes US 4–14 (UK 8–18/EU 36–46):
2yd (1.8m) fabric, 45in (112cm) wide or
1⅝yd (1.2m) fabric, 60in (152cm) wide

Sizes US 16–22 (UK 20–26/EU 48–54):
3yd (2.75m) fabric, 45in (112cm) wide or
1⅝yd (1.2m) fabric, 60in (152cm) wide

1⅛yd (1m) elastic, 1in (2.5cm) wide

Matching sewing thread

NOTE
All seam allowances are ⅜in (1cm)
unless otherwise stated

PATTERN PIECES REQUIRED
Skirt back/front
In-seam pocket

This skirt is perfect for new sewers and, with only two pattern pieces, it makes pattern matching a breeze. Once the front and back pieces of the skirt are joined, the extra width is built into the pattern to allow for the gathers at the waist and the A-line shape that will appear once the elastic is inserted.

1 Pre-wash and "press" your fabric before cutting and sewing (see page 8). Lay the fabric out with right sides facing. Cut two main skirt pieces on the fold, taking care to pattern match if necessary (see pages 10–11).

2 Transfer and mark the notches at the waist and side seams on the skirt pieces. The notches at the side seams will mark the position of the pockets. Cut out four pocket pieces (two pairs of front and back pieces). Transfer and mark the notches on the pockets.

3 Attach the in-seam pocket pieces to the side edges of the back and front pieces at the marked notches (see page 117), with right sides together.

4 Turn the pocket pieces out at the side. With right sides facing, pin, baste (tack), and stitch the skirt front and back together at the side seams, matching the pocket pieces and remembering to stitch around the outside edges of the pocket bags (see page 117).

5 With the skirt still wrong side out, fold the edge of the waist over by ¼in (6mm) and press in place. Fold over again a generous 1¼in (3cm) and stitch closed from the right side using a 1⅛in (2.7cm) seam allowance, and leaving a 2in (5cm) gap.

6 Cut a piece of elastic your waist circumference minus 2in (5cm). Attach a safety pin to one end of the elastic and thread it through the gap in the waistband, gathering the skirt as you do so. Keep hold of the other end of the elastic as you gather.

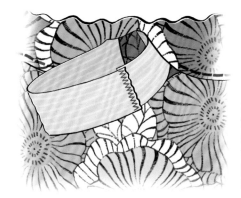

7 Once the elastic has been threaded through and the entire skirt gathered, overlap and pin both ends of the elastic together where they emerge through the gap and zig-zag stitch to secure both ends together.

8 Stitch the opening closed from the right side using a 1⅛in (2.7cm) seam allowance. At this point, the elastic should move freely inside the waistband of the skirt, allowing you to distribute the gathered fabric evenly. Once the fabric is evenly distributed, sew the elastic in place using a vertical straight stitch along both side seams of the waist.

9 To hem the skirt, with the skirt wrong side out, fold the bottom edge over by ½in (1.3cm) and press. Fold the edge over by another ½in (1.3cm), enclosing the raw edge of the fabric. Press.

10 Turn the skirt right side out to topstitch the hem in place using a ⅜in (1cm) seam allowance. Press the hem flat. Alternatively, follow this method to hem to your required length.

JENNIFER JUMPSUIT

Jumpsuits are very much on trend. This one has a dolman sleeve, which means that the bodice and sleeve are one piece, so there's no need to "set in" sleeves. Match this wardrobe essential with flats for a more dressed down look, or strappy shoes and a clutch when going out on the town!

DIFFICULTY RATING ✱ ✱ ✱

SIZES
US 4–22 (UK 8–26/EU 36–54)

FINISHED MEASUREMENTS
Length: 59½in (151cm)

MATERIALS
Sizes US 4–14 (UK 8–18/EU 36–46):
5yd (4.6m) fabric, 45in (112cm) wide or
4yd (3.6m) fabric, 60in (152cm) wide

Sizes US 16–22 (UK 20–26/EU 48–54):
6yd (5.4m) fabric, 45in (112cm) wide or
5yd (4.6m)) fabric, 60in (152cm) wide

2¼yd (2m) lining fabric

1 x 24in (61cm) invisible zipper

2¼yd (2m) bias binding, 2in (5cm) wide
(see page 120 for how to make your
own binding)

1 x hook-and-eye closure

Matching sewing thread

NOTE
The jumpsuit is slim-fitting over the hips
and thighs, so you may need to go up a
size from your usual size.

All seam allowances are ⅜in (1cm)
unless otherwise stated

PATTERN PIECES REQUIRED
Bodice front
Bodice back
Leg front
Leg back

1 Pre-wash and "press" your fabric before cutting and sewing (see page 8). Cut out all the pieces from the main fabric, pattern matching if necessary (see pages 10–11). Also cut the bodice front and back pieces from the lining fabric.

2 Next, underline the front and back bodice pieces. This means attaching the lining to the bodice and treating them as one piece as you construct the rest of the garment. Line up the front bodice outer and lining pieces, with wrong sides together. Pin, baste (tack), and sew the two pieces together around all sides. Repeat with the back bodice outer pieces and lining. You now have one lined front piece and two lined back pieces.

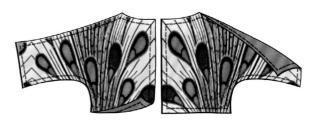

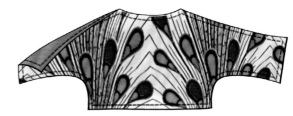

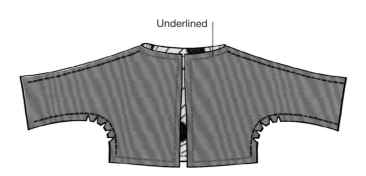

Underlined

3 Match the front and back lined bodice pieces with the right sides of the outer pieces facing. Sew together at the shoulder, arm, and side seams. Clip the underarm curve and press the seams.

4 To assemble the pants, place one leg front piece and one leg back piece with right sides together, and stitch at the side seam and inside seam. When stitching the inside seam, start at the hem and stop just before the crotch. Repeat with the second front and back pieces. You now have your left leg piece and your right leg piece.

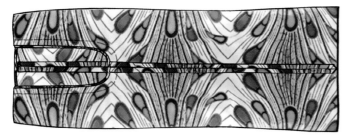

5 Next, join the legs together at the crotch. To do this, turn one leg inside out and insert it into the other leg so that the right sides are facing. Match the side seams carefully, and sew together at the crotch using a long stitch length (you will unpick some of this stitching at the back seam later when inserting the zipper).

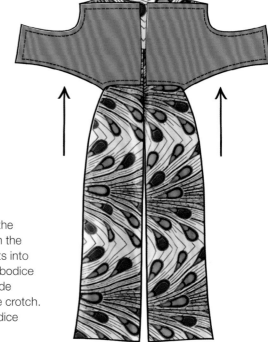

6 To attach the bodice to the pants, turn the pants right side out and lay them flat. Turn the bodice wrong side out and insert the pants into the bodice, aligning the raw edges of the bodice hem and the pants waist, matching the side seams and the center back seam with the crotch. Sew together, leaving the center back bodice seam open.

7 Turn the jumpsuit right side out. Follow the instructions on page 115 to insert the invisible zipper in the center back seam of the bodice and extending into the pants. Unpick the back crotch seam a little to accommodate the zipper. After sewing the bodice to the pants and attaching the zipper, reinforce the crotch seam by stitching over the existing seam line with a shorter stitch.

8 Attach bias binding to the neckline and sleeve hems, following the instructions on page 121. For the neckline, start and finish at the center back seam, turning the ends of the binding in by ⅜in (1cm) toward the wrong side to neaten the raw ends.

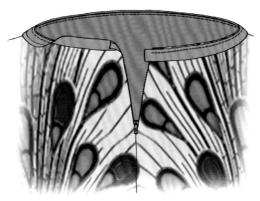

9 Finish the neck by sewing the hook-and-eye closure to the neck binding above the zipper.

10 To hem the pants, fold the bottom edge under to the wrong side by ½in (1.3cm) and press. Fold the edge under by another ½in (1.3cm), enclosing the raw edge of the fabric. Press. Topstitch from the right side taking a ½in (1.3cm) seam allowance and ensuring that the folded edge is caught in the stitching line. Press the hem flat. Alternatively, follow this method to hem to your required length.

PRISCILLA T-SHIRT

This top has no zippers or fastenings and is the perfect pattern for beginners, whether you are new to sewing, to African wax prints, or to both! Pattern matching can be tricky when sewing with wax prints, but with only two pattern pieces, pattern matching the Priscilla is a cinch!

DIFFICULTY RATING ✱

SIZES
US 4–22 (UK 8–26/EU 36–54)

FINISHED MEASUREMENTS
Length: 23½in (60cm)

MATERIALS
Sizes US 4–14 (UK 8–18/EU 36–46): 2yd (1.8m) main fabric, 45in (112cm) wide or 1yd (1m) main fabric, 60in (152cm) wide

Sizes US 16–22 (UK 20–26/EU 48–54): 3yd (2.75m) main fabric, 45in (112cm) wide or 2yd (1.8m) main fabric, 60in (152cm) wide

4½yd (4m) bias binding, 2in (5cm) wide (see Note)

Matching sewing thread

Pencil or fabric marker pen

NOTES
Either make bias binding up from the same fabric as the garment (as here) or use contrast fabric for a pop of color (see page 120 for how to make your own bias binding). You can also use store-bought bias binding.

All seam allowances are ⅜in (1cm) unless otherwise stated

This top is close-fitting over the hips. Go one size up from your usual size if necessary, and increase the size of the pleats to reduce the neckline (see page 111).

PATTERN PIECES REQUIRED
Front
Back

1 Prepare your fabric before cutting and sewing (see page 8). Transfer the front and back pattern pieces onto the fabric, including the inverted box pleat lines, taking care to pattern match if necessary (see pages 10–11).Cut out the pieces. You could increase the size of the pleats in order to reduce the size of the neckline, if necessary (see page 111).

2 Fold and press the pleats (two on the front and two on the back), pin, baste (tack), and then stitch them in place along the neckline (see pages 110-111), approximately ¼in (6mm) in from the raw edge.

3 With right sides facing, pin the front and back pieces together at the shoulder seams and side seams, then stitch the seams. Finish the raw edges and press the seams open (see page 118).

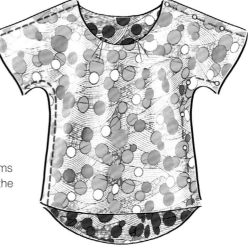

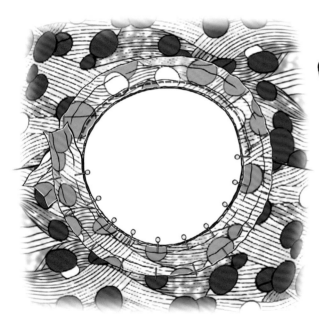

4 Turn one end of the binding over to the wrong side by ⅜in (1cm) to neaten the raw edge. Follow the instructions on page 121 to attach the binding to the neckline, pinning the binding in place all around the neck, starting at one of the shoulder seams. When you get back to the start, trim the excess binding, allowing an overlap on the end of ¾in (2cm) and tuck this under the fold. Starting from this fold, stitch around the circumference of the neckline along the opened out crease line.

5 Fold the binding back on the crease line to the inside/wrong side of the neck. Lightly press, pin, and topstitch in place from the right side along the folded edge.

6 Repeat Steps 4 and 5 to attach the binding to the sleeves and hemline in the same way to finish the top.

DIANA T-SHIRT TUNIC

This is a variation of the Priscilla top on page 22, changing it from a top into a short tunic. With the same hem and sleeves, but a little ease at the hips and some in-seam pockets, this top is a real hit! As with the Priscilla, the pleats allow you to increase or decrease the neckline to accommodate your shoulders.

DIFFICULTY RATING ✳✳

SIZES
US 4–22 (UK 8–26/EU 36–54)

FINISHED MEASUREMENTS
Length: 33in (84cm)

MATERIALS
Sizes US 4–14 (UK 8–18/EU 36–46):
3yd (2.75m) fabric, 45in (112cm) wide or
2yd (1.8m) fabric, 60in (152cm) wide

Sizes US 16–22 (UK 20–26/EU 48–54):
4yd (3.6m) fabric, 45in (112cm) wide or
3yd (2.75m) fabric, 60in (152cm) wide

2yd (1.8m) bias binding, 2in (5cm) wide
(see Note)

Matching sewing thread

Pencil or fabric marker pen

Quilting ruler

NOTES
This top is close-fitting over the hips. Go one size up from your usual size if necessary, and increase the size of the pleats to reduce the neckline (see page 111).

Either make the bias binding up from the same fabric as the garment or use contrast fabric for a pop of color as here (see page 120 for how to make your own bias binding). You can also use store-bought bias binding.

All seam allowances are ⅜in (1cm) unless otherwise stated

PATTERN PIECES REQUIRED
Front
Back
In-seam pocket

1 Pre-wash and press your fabric before cutting and sewing (see page 8). Transfer the front and back pattern pieces onto the fabric, taking care to pattern match if necessary (see pages 10–11), including the pleat lines and pocket notches. Increase the size of the pleats in order to reduce the size of the neckline, if necessary (see page 111).

2 Fold and press the pleats (two on the front and two on the back) in place, down to approximately 6–7in (15–18cm) down from the neckline, pin, and then baste (tack) them in place along the neckline (see page 111), approximately ¼in (6mm) in from the raw edge.

3 Follow the instructions on page 117 to insert the in-seam pockets. Stitch using ¼in (6mm) seam allowance, starting and stopping approximately 1in (2.5cm) above and below the pocket piece.

4 With right sides facing, pin the front and back pieces together at the shoulder seams and side seams, then stitch the seams, following the instructions on page 117 for stitching around the pocket bags. Finish the raw edges and press the seams open.

5 Attach the binding to the neckline and the ends of the sleeves, following the instructions on page 121, starting at the side seam. Trim or clip the seam allowance of the binding to half the width.

6 To hem the dress, fold the bottom edge under to the wrong side by ½in (1.3cm) and press. Fold the edge under by another ½in (1.3cm), enclosing the raw edge of the fabric. Press. Topstitch from the right side taking a ½in (1.3cm) seam allowance and ensuring that the folded edge is caught in the stitching line. Press the hem flat. Alternatively, follow this method to hem to your required length.

CHRISTIE CIRCLE SKIRT

What's not to love about this skirt? Show off the beauty of your African wax print fabric in this perfectly flared garment that oozes femininity. Once you have cut out your pieces, insert the zipper before joining the back and front pieces together and adding your waistband.

DIFFICULTY RATING ✳✳

SIZES
US 4–22 (UK 8–26/EU 36–54)

FINISHED MEASUREMENTS
Length: 30in (76cm)

MATERIALS
Sizes US 4–14 (UK 8–18/EU 36–46):
4yd (3.6m) fabric, 45in (112cm) wide or
3yd (2.75m) fabric, 60in (152cm) wide

Sizes US 16–22 (UK 20–26/EU 48–54):
5yd (4.6m) fabric, 45in (112cm) wide or
4yd (3.6m)) fabric, 60in (152cm) wide

1 x 7in (18cm) invisible zipper

approx. ½yd (50cm) lightweight iron-on interfacing for the waistband

2 x hook-and-eye closures

Matching sewing thread

NOTES
For larger sizes or for pattern matching, you may need to cut two separate pieces for the front and join them.

All seam allowances are ⅜in (1cm) unless otherwise stated

PATTERN PIECES REQUIRED
Skirt front/back
Waistband
In-seam pocket

1 Pre-wash and "press" your fabric before cutting and sewing (see page 8). Fold fabric lengthwise (across the width) and cut skirt front and backs on the crosswise grain. Baste (tack) the back pieces together along the center back seam. With right sides together, insert the invisible zipper in the skirt back (see page 115).

2 Once the zipper is inserted, remove the basting stitches and stitch the center back seam from the hem of the skirt to the end of the zipper, to close the seam and the small hole. Press the seam allowance open.

3 Attach the in-seam pocket pieces to the side edges of the back and front pieces at the marked notches (see page 117).

4 With right sides together, pin, baste, and stitch the skirt front and back together at the side seams, matching the pocket pieces and remembering to stitch around the pocket bag (see page 117).

5 Attach iron-on interfacing (see page 112) to the wrong side of the waistband piece. With right sides facing, center the waistband piece at the top of the skirt (there will be a slight overhang of approximately ½in [1.3cm] on both sides) and stitch in place. Press the seam. Turn under the excess waistband at the ends to match the circumference of the waist and to neaten the raw edges before moving on to the next step.

6 Make a ¼in (6mm) fold in the raw edge of the waistband, wrong side to the wrong side. Then turn under again so the folded edge covers the previously stitched waistband seam on the wrong side of the skirt. Pin in place, making sure that the folded edge extends beyond the waistband seam by at least ⅛in (3mm).

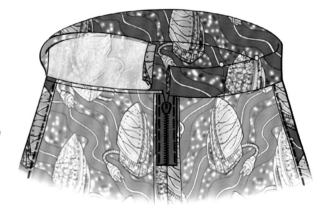

7 From the right side "stitch in the ditch" (see page 113). Close the waistband by sewing two hooks and eyes evenly spaced at the ends of the waistband and above the zipper.

8 To hem the skirt, with the skirt wrong side out, fold the bottom edge over by ½in (1.3cm) and press. Fold the edge over by another ½in (1.3cm), enclosing the raw edge of the fabric. Press. Turn the skirt right side out to topstitch the hem in place using a ½in (1.3cm) seam allowance. Press the hem flat. Alternatively, follow this method to hem to your required length.

LOTTIE CULOTTES

Easy wearing, comfortable culottes are a wardrobe staple. Smaller scale prints work best for this garment so avoid very large prints and motifs. The finished length should fall around mid-calf (depending on your height)—tailor the size of your hem accordingly.

DIFFICULTY RATING ✷✷

SIZES

US 4–22 (UK 8–26/EU 36–54)

FINISHED MEASUREMENTS

Length: 35in (89cm)

MATERIALS

Sizes US 4–14 (UK 8–18/EU 36–46):
2yd (1.8m) fabric, 45in (112cm) wide or
1yd (1m) fabric, 60in (152cm) wide

Sizes US 16–22 (UK 20–26/EU 48–54):
3yd (2.75m) fabric, 45in (112cm) wide or
2yd (1.8m) fabric, 60in (152cm) wide

1⅛yd (1m) elastic, 1in (2.5cm) wide

Safety pin

Matching sewing thread

NOTES

All seam allowances are ⅜in (1cm) unless otherwise stated

PATTERN PIECES REQUIRED

Front
Back
In-seam pocket
Waistband

1 Pre-wash and "press" your fabric before cutting and sewing (see page 8). Cut out all the pieces from the outer fabric, pattern matching if necessary (see pages 10–11). Transfer all notches.

2 Attach the in-seam pocket pieces to the side edges of the back and front pieces at the marked notches (see page 117).

3 To construct the culottes, place one front piece and one back piece with right sides together, matching the notches at the waist, and stitch at the side seam and inside seam, matching the pocket pieces and remembering to stitch around the pocket bag (see page XX). When stitching the inside seam, start at the hem and stop just before the crotch. Repeat with the second front and back pieces. You now have your left leg piece and your right leg piece.

4 Next, join the legs together at the crotch. To do this, turn one leg inside out and insert it into the other leg so that the right sides are facing. Match the side seams carefully, and sew together at the crotch (see Jennifer Jumpsuit step 5, page 20).

5 For the waistband, with right sides facing sew the short ends together using ¼in (6mm) seam allowance. With the waistband wrong side out and the culottes right side out, slip the waistband over the top of the culottes right sides together, lining up the raw edge of the waistband with the raw edge of the top waist edge of the culottes, matching the seam in the waistband with the back seam in the culottes. Pin around the circumference and stitch together.

6 With the culottes right side out, stand the waistband up and turn under the raw edge by ¼in (6mm) toward the wrong side. Press. Fold the waistband over to cover the seam joining the waistband to the culottes. Pin in place and topstitch from the right side ¼in (6mm) from the bottom edge of the waistband. Leave a 2in (5cm) gap in the stitching through which you will thread the elastic.

7 Cut a length of the elastic to your waist circumference minus 2in (5cm). Attach a safety pin to one end of the elastic and thread it through the channel in the waistband through the gap on the wrong side, taking care to keep hold of the other end of the elastic as you gather the waistband and thread the elastic through.

8 Overlap the ends of the elastic and use a zig-zag stitch to sew them together. Feel free to sew a couple of rows of zig-zag stitching to reinforce the closure. Topstitch the gap in the waistband closed from the right side.

9 To hem the culottes, fold the bottom edge under to the wrong side by ½in (1.3cm) and press. Fold the edge under by another ½in (1.3cm), enclosing the raw edge of the fabric. Press. Topstitch from the right side taking a ½in (1.3cm) seam allowance and ensuring that the folded edge is caught in the stitching line. Press the hem flat. Alternatively, follow this method to hem to your required length.

MARY SHIRT

This is an advanced make, bringing together techniques for making buttonbands and buttonholes, and adding cuffs. Once you've mastered this, why not try the Etta dress on page 54, which takes this shirt as its starting point.

DIFFICULTY RATING ✱✱✱

SIZES
US 4–22 (UK 8–26/EU 36–54)

FINISHED MEASUREMENTS
Length: 25in (63.5cm)

MATERIALS
Sizes US 4–14 (UK 8–18/EU 36–46):
2yd (1.8m) fabric, 45in (112cm) wide or
1⅛yd (1m) fabric, 60in (152cm) wide

Sizes US 16–22 (UK 20–26/EU 46–54):
3yd (2.75m) fabric, 45in (112cm) wide or
2yd (1.8m) fabric, 60in (152cm) wide

Small amount of lightweight iron-on interfacing for the collar

Carbon paper

9 x ½in (13mm) buttons

Matching sewing thread

NOTES
Pattern includes lengthening and shortening lines.

All seam allowances are ⅜in (1cm) unless otherwise stated.

PATTERN PIECES REQUIRED
Front
Back
Collar
Sleeve
Cuff

1 Pre-wash and "press" your fabric before cutting and sewing (see page 8). Transfer all notches and the pattern markings for the dart onto the front pieces of the shirt using carbon paper. Use tailor's tacks (see page 109) to mark the cross on both bodice front pieces.

2 Press the darts in place then stitch, starting at the outer edge of the piece and stopping at the point. Do not back stitch. Stitch the shirt front pieces to the back at the side seams and shoulder line, with right sides facing. Press the seams.

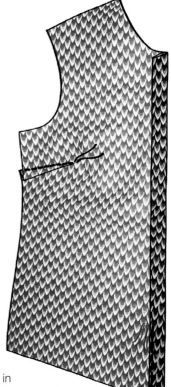

3 With wrong sides facing, turn in both center front seams on the front by ⅜in (1cm) and then by ⅜in (1cm) again. Pin in place. From a point level with the tailor's tack, topstitch the double turned edge on both sides down to the hem using a ⅜in (1cm) seam allowance. Remove the tack.

4 Clip the excess turned fabric to follow the curve of the neckline. Turn over the raw edge of the shirt neckline by ¼in (6mm), to the wrong side and topstitch in place from the right side, using ⅛in (3mm) seam allowance.

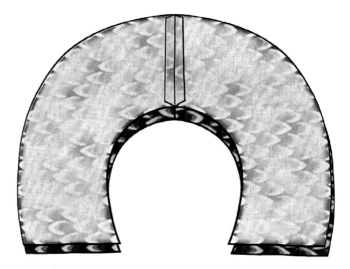

5 To construct the collar, apply the interfacing pieces (see page 112) to one pair of collar pieces then stitch them together using a ¼in (6mm) seam allowance with right sides facing on the short straight edge to make a semicircle. Press the seam open. Repeat for the other pair of collar pieces (without interfacing) so that you have two collar pieces with a central seam. The notches should be slightly closer to the front edges of the collar than the back seam.

6 Matching notches, stitch the collar pieces together with rights sides facing using a ¼in (6mm) seam allowance. Match the central seams. Leave a 2in (5cm) turning gap on the center back seam. Clip small notches (see page 119) in the seam allowance, taking care not to cut into the stitching line.

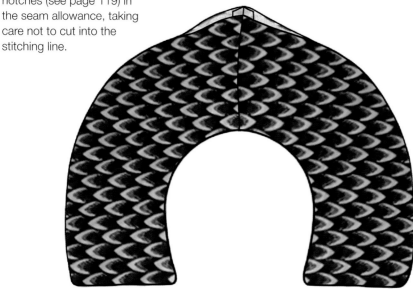

7 Turn to the right side through the gap and press, tucking under the small unstitched section. Topstitch around the edge using an edge foot or ⅛in (3mm) seam allowance, sewing the gap closed at the same time.

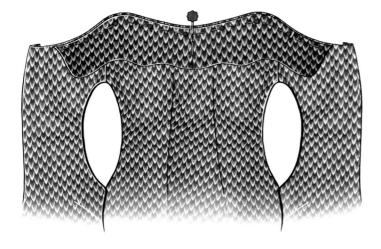

8 With the shirt right side out, mark the center back of the shirt with a pin. Pin the collar on the inside of the shirt, lining up the raw edge of the shirt with the shorter, inner curved edge of the collar and matching the notches on the collar with the notches on the bodice fronts, and the central seam on the collar with the marker pin. Stitch in place on the inside. This can be hard to imagine but remember that the collar will ultimately be flipped over to the back, thereby concealing the seam. Topstitch the collar to the seam allowance close to the seam to keep the collar lying flat.

9 Mark the buttonhole positions on the right front piece of the shirt (for women's clothing, the buttons are on the left). Use a pin to mark a point ¾in (2cm) up from the stitching at the bottom of the shirt front (where the tailor's tack was positioned). From the top of the neckline, mark a point ¾in (2cm) down using a pin. Between these two positions, evenly space out 9 buttonholes. To mark your spaces, knot a double thread and pull the needle through the buttonhole position from the right side of the shirt to the wrong side, approximately ½in (1.3cm) from the folded edge. Stitch the buttonholes following your sewing machine's instructions (see pages 121-122.)

10 Hand sew the buttons onto the left-hand side (see page 122.) Take care lining up buttons with their respective buttonholes. Position the buttons approximately ¼in (6mm) from the folded edge.

11 Before stitching the sleeves, use tailor's tacks to mark the center point at the top of the sleeve (the sleeve head). Note the back of the sleeve is indicated by a double notch and the front of the sleeve is indicated by a single notch. Sew two rows of long stitches between the notches, no more than ¼in (6mm) from the top of the sleeve, and leave long thread ends at each end. Pull these ends to create gathers at the top of the sleeve. Sew the sleeve piece right sides together at the sides. Press, clip, and trim the seam. Repeat so that you have two sleeves.

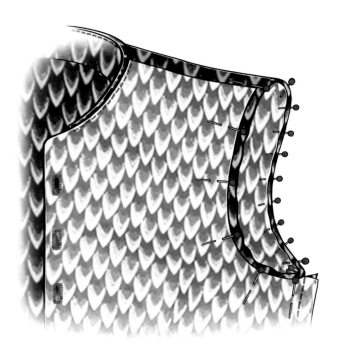

12 Turn the shirt wrong side out. With the sleeve right side out, insert the sleeve into the armhole with right sides facing, matching the center seam of the sleeve with the side seam of the shirt. Match notches so that the back of the sleeve is facing the back of the shirt and the front of the sleeve is facing the front. Ease the gathering evenly to fit the armhole, then pin the sleeve in place, starting at the center seam and working outward. Take your time with this and use as many pins as you need. Stitch using a ⅝in (1.5cm) seam allowance. Remove the rows of gathering stitches.

13 Apply the interfacing to both cuff pieces (see page 112). Fold in half lengthwise, with right sides facing. Stitch the short edges together. Press. Turn the cuff right side out with the raw edges level. Repeat with the other cuff.

14 Stitch two rows around the hem of the sleeve using a long stitch length, no more than ¼in (6mm) from the end of the sleeve, and leave long thread ends at each end. Pull these ends to create gathers, which will create fullness just above the hem and reduce the circumference of the sleeve hem. Gather the end of the sleeve to the same circumference as the cuff, and spread the gathers out evenly around the hem.

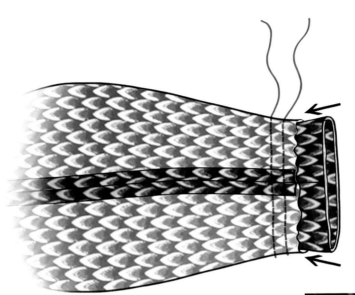

15 Turn the sleeve wrong side out. Insert the cuff into the sleeve, right sides facing, so that the raw edge of the cuff matches the raw edge of the sleeve hem. Match the seams and stitch together. Remove the two rows of gathering stitches. Pull the cuff and sleeve right side out and your cuff has been attached. Repeat with the other sleeve.

16 With the shirt wrong side out, fold the raw edge of the shirt hem over by ⅜in (1cm) and press. Fold the edge over by another ⅜in (1cm), enclosing the raw edge. Turn the shirt right side out to topstitch the hem in place using a ⅜in (1cm) seam allowance. Press the hem flat. Alternatively, follow this method to hem to your required length.

MEGHAN TUNIC DRESS

This boatneck shift style is an absolute wardrobe staple that is stylish yet versatile. The possibilities with this make are endless: use contrasting binding and patch pockets for casual wear or match them all in the same fabric for a working wardrobe classic.

DIFFICULTY RATING ✷✷

SIZES
US 4–22 (UK 8–26/EU 36–54)

FINISHED MEASUREMENTS
Length: 41in (104cm)

MATERIALS
Sizes US 4–14 (UK 8–18/EU 36–46):
4yd (3.6m) fabric, 45in (112cm) wide or 3yd (2¾m) fabric, 60in (152cm) wide

Sizes US 16–22 (UK 20–26/EU 48–54):
5yd (4.6m) fabric, 45in (112cm) wide or 4yd (3.6m) fabric, 60in (152cm) wide

½yd (50cm) contrasting fabric for pockets (if using)

Carbon paper

Fusible adhesive (optional)

2yd (1.8m) bias binding, 3in (7½cm) wide (see page 120 for how to make your own bias binding)

Matching sewing thread

NOTES
All seam allowances are ⅜in (1cm) unless otherwise stated

PATTERN PIECES REQUIRED
Front
Back
Patch pocket

1 Pre-wash and "press" your fabric before cutting and sewing (see page 8). Cut out the pattern pieces. Trace the patch pocket position markings onto the right side of the front using carbon paper (but do not mark the top line of the pocket). Make two patch pockets following the instructions on page 116.

2 Position the patch pockets using the placement lines on the right side of the front piece. Use pins or thin strips of fusible adhesive at the bottom edge and side edges of the pocket to temporarily fix the pockets in place while sewing. Keep the adhesive strip within the ¼in (6mm) seam allowance. Topstitch in place from the right side. Remove the adhesive strips.

3 Trace the bust darts using carbon paper onto the wrong side of the front of the dress piece. Press the darts in place then stitch, starting at the outer edge of the piece and stopping at the point. Do not back stitch. Press the dart down toward the dress hem. Do this from the wrong side first and then press from the right side. Use a tailor's ham if you have one.

4 With right sides together, pin, baste, and stitch the front and back dress pieces together at the side seams and shoulder seams.

5 Turn the dress right side out. Attach bias binding to the neckline and armhole edges, starting at the shoulder seams and folding the end of the opened-out binding over by ¾in (2cm), pin in place then sew, following the instructions on page 121.

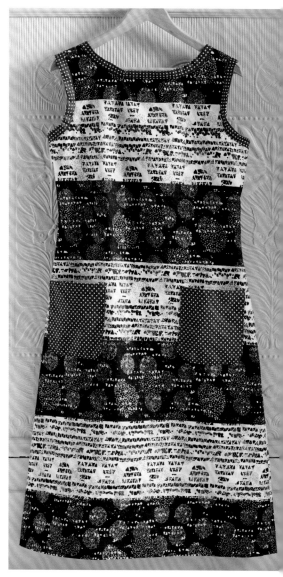

6 To hem the dress, fold the bottom edge under to the wrong side by ½in (1.3cm) and press. Fold the edge under by another ½in (1.3cm), enclosing the raw edge of the fabric. Press. Topstitch from the right side taking a ½in (1.3cm) seam allowance and ensuring that the folded edge is caught in the stitching line. Press the hem flat. Alternatively, follow this method to hem to your required length.

PHILIPPA PINAFORE

Pinafores are a perfect wardrobe staple and the mixing and matching possibilities are endless. Don't be afraid to try bold colors that you can then tone down with solid-color tops, shirts, and sweaters. For the colder months, pair with cotton leggings and boots and you are good to go.

DIFFICULTY RATING ✷✷✷

SIZES
US 4–22 (UK 8–26/EU 36–54)

FINISHED MEASUREMENTS
Length: 38¼in (97cm)

MATERIALS
4yd (3.6m) fabric, 45in (112cm) wide or 3yd (2.7m) fabric, 60in (152cm) wide

1⅛yd (1m) lining fabric

½yd (½m) lightweight iron-on interfacing (or enough from your scraps to interface 4 strap pieces)

Carbon paper

Matching sewing thread

Fusible adhesive (optional)

Elastic for your individual back waist measurement (half your waist circumference), 2in (5cm) wide

NOTES
All seam allowances are ⅜in (1cm) unless otherwise stated

PATTERN PIECES REQUIRED
Bodice front
Bodice back
Skirt front
Skirt back
Back waistband
Strap
Patch pocket

1 Pre-wash and "press" your fabric before cutting and sewing (see page 8). Cut out the pattern pieces from the main fabric, taking care to pattern match if necessary (see pages 10–11). Also cut the Front bodice and Back bodice from the lining fabric. Trace the patch pocket position markings onto the right side of the skirt front. When transferring the pocket markings, only trace the sides and the bottom lines, not the top line, if using carbon paper or any other permanent marking tool, as the top line will remain visible after the pocket has been attached.

2 Apply the interfacing to all four strap pieces on the wrong side. Sew two interfaced strap pieces together with right sides facing, taking a ¼in (6mm) seam allowance, sewing the sides and one long edge and leaving a 2in (5cm) gap on the opposite long edge. Clip all four corners. Turn the strap right side out and slip stitch to close the gap. Press. Repeat with the remaining strap pieces to make a second strap.

3 Next, you will "bag out" the bodice front. To do this, pin the bodice front outer and lining pieces together with right sides facing and pin, baste (tack), and stitch at the armholes, side seams, and the top of the front bodice, leaving the bottom edge unstitched. "Bag out" the bodice by turning right side out through the gap. Put the front bodice to one side.

4 The back bodice is sewn slightly differently. Take the two back waistband pieces and attach one to the outer back bodice with right sides together, matching the raw edges. Attach the remaining waistband to the back lining piece. Press the seams.

5 Next, stitch these back pieces together with right sides facing at the side seams and armholes, leaving the top and bottom of the back bodice unstitched. Insert the finished straps between the back outer fabric and lining fabric, so that the ends are lined up with top of the bodice, using notches to position them accurately.

6 Stitch along the bodice top to secure the straps in place. Clip the armhole seams around the curve, then turn right side out. Stitch the lined bodice back and lined bodice front pieces to each other with right sides facing, at the armhole and the side seams—the hems of both bodice pieces (front and back) remain unstitched.

7 Make two patch pockets following the instructions on page 116. Position the patch pockets using the placement lines on the right side of the front skirt. Use pins or thin strips of fusible adhesive at the bottom edge and side edges of the pocket to temporarily fix the pockets in place while sewing. Keep the adhesive strip within the ¼in (6mm) seam allowance. Topstitch in place from the right side. Remove the adhesive strips. Stitch the skirt front to the skirt back at the side seams.

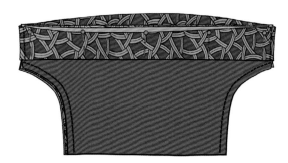

8 Cut the elastic to measure your back waist measurement (half your waist measurement) minus 1in (2.5cm). Insert the length of elastic into the back bodice waistband. At this stage, the hem in the lower edge of the waistband on the back bodice is open, so simply insert the elastic into the gap, centered on the length. Pin and stitch in place at the raw edge of the waistband using a ¼in (6mm) seam allowance. Make sure the straps are tucked out of the way.

9 With the skirt right side out and the bodice wrong side out, insert the skirt into the bodice right sides facing, aligning the raw edges of the bodice hem and the skirt waist. Pin, baste, and stitch together then turn the completed pinafore right side out.

10 Insert the snap fasteners at the top of the bodice and the end of the straps, following the manufacturer's instructions. You can adjust the position of the snaps to your own fit.

11 To hem the skirt, fold the bottom edge under to the wrong side by ½in (1.3cm) and press. Fold the edge under by another ½in (1.3cm), enclosing the raw edge of the fabric. Press. Topstitch from the right side taking a ½in (1.3cm) seam allowance and ensuring that the folded edge is caught in the stitching line. Press the hem flat. Alternatively, follow this method to hem to your required length.

TIP
Use a chalk mark to help you to identify the right or wrong side of your fabric if they are very similar.

DOROTHY TUNIC DRESS

The Dorothy is a more formal version of the Meghan (see page 44), with added sleeves. These sleeves come in two parts: the top sleeve, which stops at the elbow and then the bottom bell sleeve. Make up the garment entirely in your outer fabric or use contrast fabric for the bell sleeve, patch pockets, and neckline binding, as you prefer.

DIFFICULTY RATING ✱✱✱

SIZES
US 4–22 (UK 8–26/EU 36–54)

FINISHED MEASUREMENTS
Finished back length: 41in (104cm)

MATERIALS
Sizes US 4–14 (UK 8–18/EU 36–46):
5yd (4.6m) fabric, 45in (112cm) wide or
4yd (3.6m) fabric, 60in (152cm) wide

Sizes US 16–22 (UK 20–26/EU 48–54):
6yd (5.4m) fabric, 45in (112cm) wide or
5yd (4.6m) fabric, 60in (152cm) wide

1⅛yd (1m) contrasting fabric (optional for pockets, binding, bell sleeve)

Carbon paper

Fusible adhesive (optional)

½yd (0.5m) bias binding, 2in (5cm) wide for neckline (see page 120 for how to make your own bias binding)

Matching sewing thread

NOTES
All seam allowances are ⅜in (1cm) unless otherwise stated

PATTERN PIECES REQUIRED
Meghan front
Meghan back
Sleeve top
Sleeve bottom
Patch pocket

1 Follow steps 1–4 of the Meghan Tunic on pages 45–46 to construct the main body of the tunic with patch pockets attached.

2 Turn the tunic right side out. Attach bias binding to the neckline only, starting at the shoulder seams and folding the end of the opened-out binding over by ¾in (2cm), pin in place then sew, following the instructions on page 121.

3 For the sleeves, sew the side seams of each piece together with right sides facing, so that you have two sleeve tops and two flounces. Note the back of the top sleeve is indicated by a double notch and the front of the sleeve is indicated by a single notch.

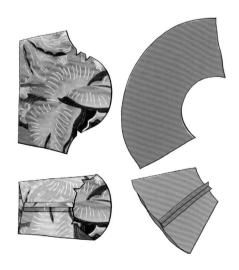

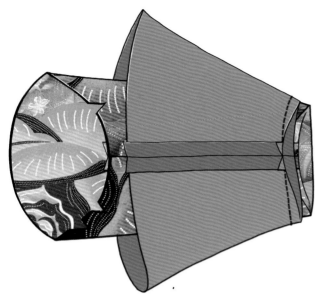

4 To attach the sleeve top to the bell sleeve, turn the sleeve top right side out and insert it into the bell sleeve, which is still wrong side out. Match raw edges and the center seams. Pin, baste (tack), and stitch together. Press, clip, and trim the seam. Repeat for the remaining pieces. You now have two completed sleeves.

5 Turn the tunic wrong side out and the sleeve right side out. Insert one sleeve into the tunic armhole, matching the center seam of the sleeve with the side seam of the tunic, match the notches to ensure that the back of the sleeve is facing the back of the tunic and the front of the sleeve is facing the front of the tunic. Check that the sleeve and tunic are right sides facing and the bell sleeve is positioned down inside the tunic. Pin in place starting at the side seam of the dress and working outward. Take your time with this and use as many pins as you need. Sew carefully.

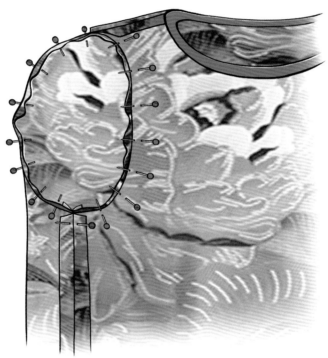

6 To finish the flounce, fold the edge under to the wrong side by ¼in (6mm) and press. Fold the edge under by another ¼in (6mm), enclosing the raw edge of the fabric. Press. Topstitch from the right side taking a ⅛in (3mm) seam allowance and ensuring that the folded edge is caught in the stitching line. Press flat.

7 To hem the dress, fold the bottom edge under to the wrong side by ½in (1.3cm) and press. Fold the edge under by another ½in (1.3cm), enclosing the raw edge of the fabric. Press. Topstitch from the right side taking a ½in (1.3cm) seam allowance and ensuring that the folded edge is caught in the stitching line. Press the hem flat. Alternatively, follow this method to hem to your required length.

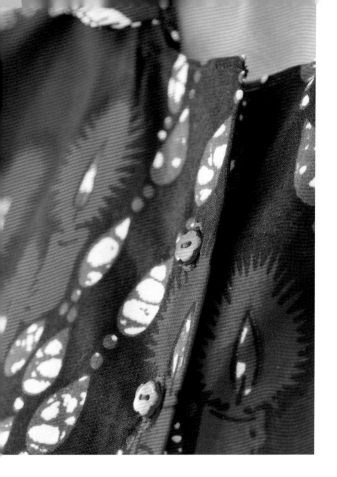

ETTA SLEEVELESS SHIRT DRESS

This dress takes the Mary shirt on page 36 as its starting point, but the shirt-style top is sleeveless and more closely fitted, and I've added a button-through skirt to make a chic spring or summer day dress. When using fabric with directional prints or motifs, take extra care when cutting out so that the designs are pointing the same way.

DIFFICULTY RATING ✱✱✱

SIZES

US 4–22 (UK 8–26/EU 36–54)

FINISHED MEASUREMENTS

Finished back length: 37in (94cm)

MATERIALS

Sizes US 4–14 (UK 8–18/EU 36–46): 5yd (4.6m) fabric, 45in (112cm) wide or 4yd (3.6m) fabric, 60in (152cm) wide

Sizes US 16–22 (UK 20–26/EU 48–54): 6yd (5.5m) fabric, 45in (112cm) wide or 5yd (4.6m) fabric, 60in (152cm) wide

¼yd (25cm) lightweight iron-on interfacing

15 x ½in (13mm) buttons

Matching sewing thread

NOTES

Pattern includes lengthening and shortening lines.

All seam allowances are ⅜in (1cm) unless otherwise stated

PATTERN PIECES REQUIRED

Bodice front
Bodice back
Skirt front
Skirt back
Mary collar

1 Pre-wash and "press" your fabric before cutting and sewing (see page 8). Transfer all notches and the pattern markings for the dart onto the front pieces of the bodice using carbon paper.

2 Press the darts in place then stitch, starting at the outer edge of the piece and stopping at the point (see page 110). Do not back stitch. Stitch the bodice front pieces to the bodice back at the side seams and shoulder line, with right sides facing. Press the seams.

3 Stitch the skirt front pieces to the back at the side seams, with right sides facing. Press the seams. The center front of both bodice and skirt are open. Stitch the skirt to the bodice with right sides facing and matching the side seams.

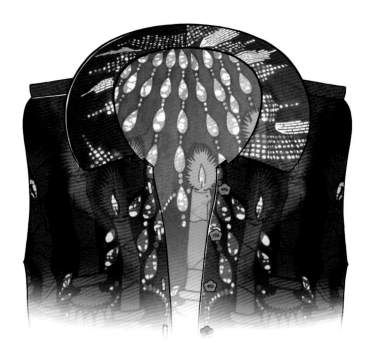

4 Follow steps 3–8 in Mary shirt project (pages 36–39 and stitch the button band on both center front edges and construct and attach the collar. Use a pin to mark a point ¾in (2cm) up from the stitching at the lower edge of the skirt button band. From the top of the neckline, mark a point ¾in (2cm) down using a pin. Between these two positions, evenly space out 15 buttonholes. Follow steps 9–10 on page 39 to sew the buttonholes, following your sewing machine instructions, and attach the buttons.

5 With the dress wrong side out, hem the armhole edge using a narrow hem. Turn the armhole edge to the wrong side by ¼in (6mm), fold again by ¼in (6mm). Topstitch using an edge foot or ⅛in (3mm) from the edge.

6 With the dress wrong side out, fold the bottom edge over by ½in (1.3cm) and press. Fold the edge over by another ½in (1.3cm), enclosing the raw edge. Turn the dress right side out to topstitch the hem in place using a ½in (1.3cm) seam allowance and ensuring that the folded edge is caught in the stitching line. Press the hem flat. Alternatively, follow this method to hem to your required length.

MILLIE DRESS

With its one-piece sleeve, the bodice from the Jennifer Jumpsuit on page 18 is an absolute keeper! This pattern sees that bodice twinned with a fitted skirt, transforming the jumpsuit into an ideal outfit for date nights, parties, and other special occasions.

DIFFICULTY RATING ✱✱

SIZES
US 4–22 (UK 8–26/EU 36–54)

FINISHED MEASUREMENTS
Finished back length: 45in (114.3cm)

MATERIALS
Sizes US 4–14 (UK 8–18/EU 36–46):
5yd (4.6m) fabric, 45in (112cm) wide or
4yd (3.6m) fabric, 60in (152cm) wide

Sizes US 16–22 (UK 20–26/EU 48–54):
6yd (5.5m) fabric, 45in (112cm) wide or
5yd (4.6m) fabric, 60in (152cm) wide

2¼yd (2m) lining fabric

24in (61cm) invisible zipper

2¼yd (2m) bias binding, 2in (5cm) wide
(see page 120 for how to make your
own bias binding)

1 x hook-and-eye closure

Matching sewing thread

NOTES
Pattern includes lengthening and shortening lines.

All seam allowances are ⅜in (1cm) unless otherwise stated

PATTERN PIECES REQUIRED
Jennifer bodice front
Jennifer bodice back
Skirt front
Skirt back

1 Pre-wash and "press" your fabric before cutting and sewing (see page 8). Cut out all the pieces from the main fabric, pattern matching if necessary (see pages 10–11), and cut the bodice front and back from the lining fabric.

2 Next, follow the instructions for steps 1–3 of the Jennifer Jumpsuit on pages 19–20 to underline the front and back bodice pieces, then sew them together. Clip the underarm curve and press the seams.

3 To construct the skirt, place the front piece and the two back pieces with right sides together, and stitch at the side seams. Stitch the center back seam using a long stitch length, as you will unpick some of the seam to insert the zipper.

4 To attach the bodice to the skirt, turn the skirt right side out and lay it flat. Turn the bodice wrong side out and insert the skirt into the bodice, aligning the raw edges of the bodice hem and the skirt waist, matching the side seams and the center back seam. Sew together, leaving the center back bodice seam open.

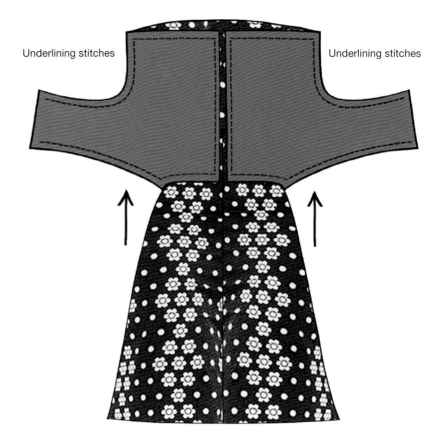

Underlining stitches   Underlining stitches

5 Turn the dress right side out. Follow the instructions on page 115 to insert the invisible zipper in the center back seam of the bodice and extending into the skirt. Pin the opened zipper in place on the left side from the top downward to the end of the zipper. Carefully unpick some of the long stitches on the skirt back seam of the dress starting from the skirt waist.

6 Follow the instructions on page 115 to finish inserting the zipper, and stitch in place, ensuring that your stitches are not too close to the zipper teeth. Starting from the hem, restitch the seam from the bottom of the zipper to the hem, starting the stitching as close as possible to the end of your invisible zipper.

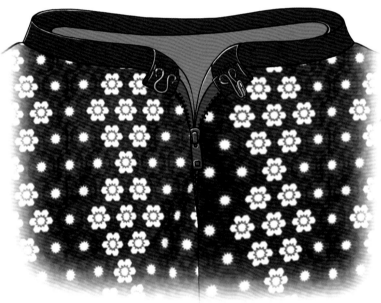

7 Attach bias binding to the neckline and sleeve hems, following the instructions on page 121. For the neckline, start and finish at the center back seam, turning the ends of the binding in by ⅜in (1cm) to neaten the raw ends. Finish the neck by sewing the hook-and-eye closure to the neck binding above the zipper.

8 To hem the skirt, fold the bottom edge under to the wrong side by ½in (1.3cm) and press. Fold the edge under by another ½in (1.3cm), enclosing the raw edge of the fabric. Press and pin in place. Topstitch from the right side taking a ½in (1.3cm) seam allowance and ensuring that the folded edge is caught in the stitching line. Press the hem flat. Alternatively, follow this method to hem to your required length.

BETSY DRESS

This dress has a lapped zip and set-in, gathered sleeves that may test your skills but it's perfect for showing off really large motifs and is sure to turn heads! The full length sleeves with gathered ends add a chic touch.

DIFFICULTY RATING ✳✳✳

SIZES
US 4–22 (UK 8–26/EU 36–54)

FINISHED MEASUREMENTS
Finished back length: 43in (109cm)

MATERIALS
Sizes US 4–14 (UK 8–18/EU 36–46):
5yd (4.6m) fabric, 45in (112cm) wide or
4yd (3.6m) fabric, 60in (152cm) wide

Sizes US 16–22 (UK 20–26/EU 48–54):
6yd (5.4m) fabric, 45in (112cm) wide or
5yd (4.6m) fabric, 60in (152cm) wide

1⅛yd (1m) bias binding 2in (5cm) wide (see page 120 for how to make your own bias binding.)

Small amount of lightweight iron-on interfacing for cuffs

Carbon paper

Matching sewing thread

22in (56cm) zipper

Zipper foot

Chalk

NOTE
All seam allowances are ⅜in (1cm) unless otherwise stated

PATTERN PIECES REQUIRED
Front
Back
Sleeve
Cuff
In-seam pocket

1 Pre-wash and "press" your fabric before cutting and sewing (see page 8), pattern matching if necessary (see pages 10–11). Transfer any notches to the fabric pieces.

2 Press the darts in place then stitch, starting at the outer edge of the piece and stopping at the point (see page 110). Do not back stitch.

3 Follow the instructions on page 117 to attach the in-seam pockets, starting and stopping approximately 1in (2.5cm) above and below the pocket piece.

4 With right sides facing, pin the front and back pieces together at the shoulder seams and side seams, then stitch the seams, following the instructions on page 117 for stitching around the pocket bags. Finish the raw edges and press the seams open.

5 With the dress wrong side out and the back facing you, draw a chalk line ¾in (2cm) in from the raw edge of the center back piece. Repeat on the opposite side. The length of the line should match the length of your zipper.

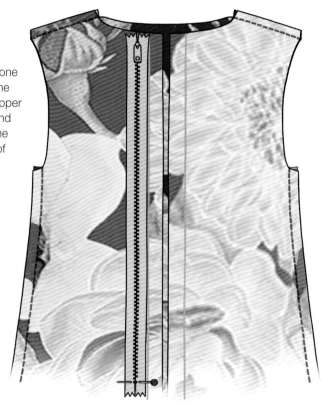

6 Place the zipper right side up, parallel to one of the chalk lines, with the zipper tape on the outside of the line. Line up the top of the zipper with the raw edge at the top of the dress and pin. Importantly, use a pin to mark where the silver colored tab is located at the bottom of the zipper.

7 Remove the zipper and put it to one side. Join the two back pieces together with right sides facing, stitching down from the point marked with a pin at the bottom of the zipper to the hem, taking a ¾in (2cm) seam allowance.

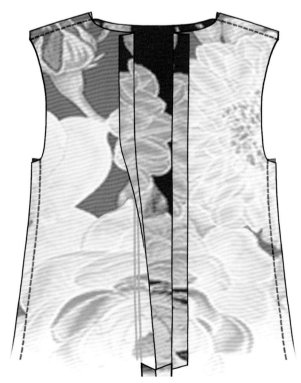

8 Draw a second chalk line on the left side only, ⅛in (3mm) out from the first chalk line toward the raw edge. Fold over the raw edge to the wrong side along this line. On the other side edge, fold along the single chalk line to the wrong side and press.

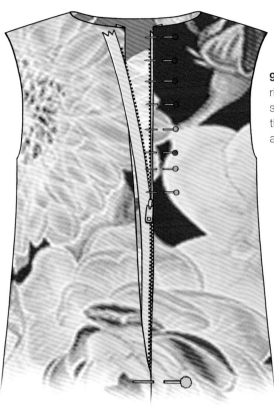

9 Turn the dress right side out. Place the zipper right side up underneath the open center back seam and pin on the right-hand edge, ensuring that the zipper teeth are visible along the edge and opening the zipper halfway.

10 When you get to the halfway point of your zipper, pull the zipper up to the top and continue pinning to the end of your zipper right down to the silver metal stop. Topstitch from the right side using an edge foot or ⅛in (3mm) seam allowance (use the left side of zipper foot to sew right side of zipper).

11 Place the larger, lapped side over the topstitched line on the right of the zipper to cover the stitching. Pin in place along this edge to hold it securely, placing the pins parallel to the edge. Add a second line of pins to mark a stitch line ½in (1.3cm) in from the lapped edge (over the left-hand edge of the zipper tape beneath). Stitch, using this second line of pins as a guide. Remove the pins and your lapped zipper is complete.

12 Follow the instructions on page 121 to attach bias binding to the neckline, starting at the shoulder seams.

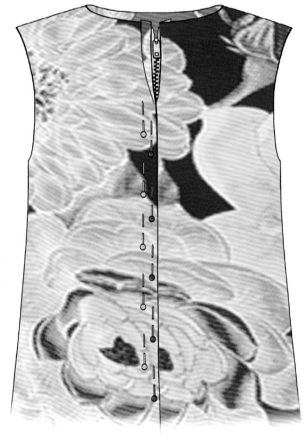

13 For the sleeves, note that the back of the sleeve is indicated by a double notch and the front of the sleeve is indicated by a single notch. In order to create gathers at the sleeve head along the top of the sleeve, use a long stitch length to stitch two rows of stitching between the notches. Before you start stitching remember to keep your thread ends nice and long. Stitch the first line ⅜in (1cm) from the raw edge and the second line ¼in (6mm) from the raw edge. Repeat for the other sleeve piece. Sew a single line of gathering stitches at the hem, ¼in (6mm) from the edge, leaving long thread ends at the start and end.

14 Sew the sleeve right sides together at the side seam. Press the seam open. Slowly begin to create gathers at the sleeve head by pulling the long thread ends of your long stitching lines.

15 Turn the dress wrong side out and the sleeves right side out. Insert one sleeve into the armhole, matching the center seam of sleeve with the side seam of the dress, and match the notches to ensure that the back of the sleeve is facing the back of the dress and the front of the sleeve is facing the front of the dress. Carefully continue to ease gathers within the armhole by gently pulling on the thread ends, making the sleeve head smaller or larger so that it fits the circumference of the armhole.

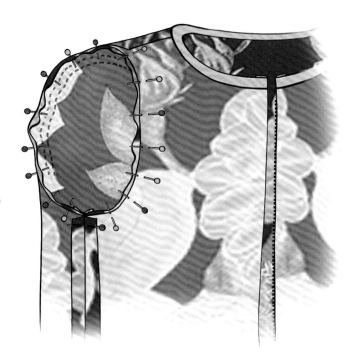

16 Pin in place starting at the center seam and working outward. Take your time with this and use as many pins as you need. Stitch together using a ⅝in (1.5cm) seam allowance. Pull the sleeve to the right side to make sure that your gathers are even. Remove the lines of stitching used to create the gathers. Repeat with the other sleeve.

17 Follow the instructions in steps 13–15 of the Mary Shirt on pages 40–41 to construct the cuff, gather the bottom of the sleeve, and insert the cuff, using a ⅜in (1cm) seam allowance, ensuring that the gathered end matches the circumference of the cuff.

18 With the dress wrong side out, fold the hem over by ½in (1.3cm) and press. Fold the hem over by another ½in (1.3cm), enclosing the raw edge of the fabric. Turn the tunic right side out to topstitch the hem in place using a ⅜in (1cm) seam allowance. Press the hem flat. Alternatively, follow this method to hem to your required length.

BEATRICE TOTE BAG

This is a great project for your first attempt at bag-making, and is ideal for using smaller scale prints. Follow the instructions for the pattern piece sizes and plot them directly onto your fabric before cutting out.

DIFFICULTY RATING ✱✱

FINISHED MEASUREMENTS
Height (excluding handles): 16in (40½cm)

Width: 14in (35½cm)

MATERIALS
1⅛yd (1m) outer fabric, 45in (112cm) wide

1⅛yd (1m) fusible fleece

1⅛yd (1m) lightweight iron-on interfacing

½yd (½m) lining fabric, 45in (112cm) wide

1 x metal no-sew snap closure

Matching sewing thread

CUTTING GUIDE
Cut 2 of the following in each of outer fabric, interfacing, and fusible fleece:

Main bag: 15 x 17in (38 x 43cm)
Facing: 15 x 3½in (38 x 9cm)

Cut 2 of the following in each of lining and interfacing:
Lining: 15 x 14½in (38 x 37cm)

Cut 2 of the following in each of outer fabric and interfacing:

Handles: 26 x 4in (66 x 10cm)

NOTE
All seam allowances are ⅜in (1cm) unless otherwise stated

1 Cut the pattern pieces following the cutting guide. For the main bag and facing, fuse the interfacing (see page 112) and the fleece to the wrong side of the outer bag fabric; lay the interfacing onto the wrong side of the fabric before the fleece but be sure to fuse both together at the same time. Keep any spare fusible fleece to reinforce the snap closure.

2 For the lining, cut two 15 x 14½in (38 x 37cm) pieces in lining fabric and interfacing only (no fleece). Fuse the interfacing to the wrong side of the lining pieces. For the handles, cut two 26 x 4in (66 x 10cm) pieces from the outer fabric and interfacing (no fleece), and fuse the interfacing to the wrong side of the handle pieces.

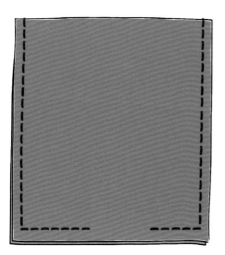

3 With right sides together, pin, baste (tack), and stitch the (longer) side seams and (shorter) bottom of the outer bag pieces. Sew the lining pieces along the longer side seams. Do not sew the bottom seam of the lining closed. Instead, only sew 1½in (4cm) and 2in (5cm) in from each of the side seams of the lining and backstitch at both ends. You will use this gap to turn the bag through at the end. Press the seams open.

4 Next, create a box shape for the bottom of the bag in both the lining and outer fabric pieces. Take a corner and pull the fabric out to either side to create a triangular point with the seam running down the center. Make sure the seams are aligned. Mark a line across the triangle, 2½in (6cm) down from the tip, and pin to keep the layers together. Stitch across the line, then trim off the tip about ¼in (6mm) from the stitched line. Repeat for each corner in the lining and outer fabric.

5 To assemble the handles, press each piece in half lengthwise, wrong sides together. Open the pieces and press each outside edge toward the center line. Fold the fabric strip in half lengthwise. Press.

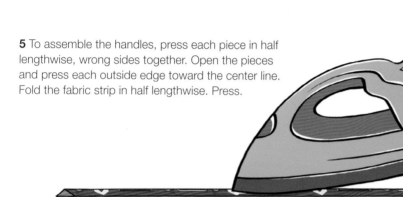

6 Topstitch each long side of the handle, close to the edge, using a ¼in (6mm) machine foot. Neaten the ends of the handles as necessary using embroidery scissors.

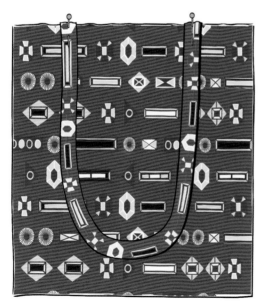

7 Turn the outer bag right side out. To attach the handles to the bag, mark 3in (8cm) in from both side seams on the right side of the back and front outer bag. Pin the ends of the handles at the marked positions, lining up the raw edges of the handles with the raw edges at the top of the bag (right side to right side), ensuring that the handles are not twisted.

8 Now mark the center on the wrong side of both facing pieces for the position of the snap closures. Take your time to make sure you position your mark accurately as you will use this as a guide to insert both sides of the snap closure. Then, stitch the two pieces of facing together right side to right side at the short ends to make a circle.

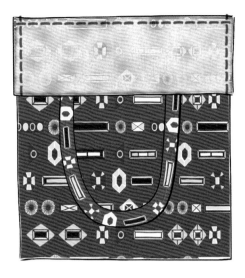

9 Slip the facing over the top of the bag, right side to right side, leaving the handles sandwiched between the facing and the bag. Line up all raw edges, pin, baste, and stitch in place. Pull the facing upward and understitch the facing only to the bag/facing seam allowance, ¼in (6mm) from the raw edge. Turn the facing to the inside then topstitch on the right side to finish, ¼in (6mm) from the top edge.

10 Turn the bag wrong side out and follow the manufacturer's instructions to attach the snap closure to the right side of the facing, using the marks made in Step 8 on the wrong side as a guide. Make a hole at the marked position using an awl or seam ripper, and push the pronged cover through from right side to wrong side. Use any spare pieces of fusible fleece cut to the diameter of the snap to reinforce the facing at the point where the closures are attached, pushing the fleece over the prongs before securing the snap.

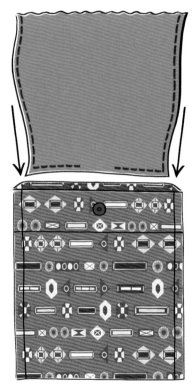

11 With the lining piece right side out, insert the lining into the outer bag with right sides facing (keeping the outer bag wrong side out). Tuck the handles in between the outer bag and lining, out of the way. Lift up the facing and stitch the raw edge of the facing to the raw edge of the lining.

12 Then, the fun bit! Carefully, turn the outer fabric to the right side through the gap in the bottom of the lining. Marvel at your creation and then use a matching thread to slip stitch the gap in the lining closed.

PENNY COIN PURSE

This simple-sew coin purse is a great stash buster—why not use leftover fabric from the Beatrice Tote Bag on page 70 to make a matching set? It's perfect for keeping all your loose change and other small items together so they don't end up at the bottom of your bag!

FINISHED MEASUREMENTS

Height: 5½in (14cm)

Width: 5½in (14cm)

MATERIALS

¼yd (25cm) outer fabric

¼yd (25cm) fusible fleece,

¼yd (25cm) lining fabric,

¼yd (25cm) lightweight iron-on interfacing

1 x 7in (18cm) zipper

Matching sewing thread

CUTTING GUIDE

Cut 6in (15cm) squares:

2 x outer fabric

2 x lining fabric

4 x iron-on interfacing

2 x fusible fleece

NOTES

All seam allowances are ⅜in (1cm) unless otherwise stated

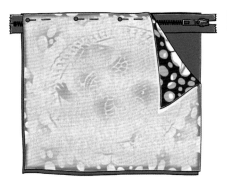 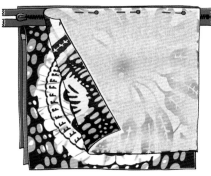

1 Fuse one piece of interfacing (see page 112) and one piece of fleece to the wrong side of each of the outer fabric pieces and one piece of interfacing to the wrong side of each of the lining pieces.

2 Lay one square of lining with the right side facing you. Place the zipper on the top of the lining, face up, along the top edge, then place the outer fabric on top, right side facing down. With all raw edges aligned, pin the three layers together with the zipper sandwiched in between.

3 Stitch in place using a zipper foot, keeping the stitches close to the zipper teeth. Fold back the outer and lining so that the wrong sides are together and the other side of the zipper is revealed. Repeat Step 2 to attach the remaining outer and lining pieces on the other side of the zipper.

4 Fold back the attached fabric pairs so that the zipper is in the middle, with the outer fabric facing up and the lining underneath. Press the fabric next to the zipper and then topstitch along both sides of the zipper using matching thread.

5 Next, lay both outer pieces together, right sides facing, and take to one side, and repeat with the lining pieces to the other side. Open the zipper approximately 4in (10cm); you will use this opening later to pull the completed purse through to the right side. Stitch all around the edge of the purse, leaving a 4in (10cm) gap in the lining. Trim excess fabric close to the seam allowance at the corners and any excess zipper tape at either end.

6 Reach through the gap in the lining and zipper to pull the purse through to the right side. Slip stitch the gap in the lining using a matching thread, then push the lining back inside the purse, pushing the corners out carefully.

CORINNE PENCIL CASE

This makes a perfect gift for students of any age, and can be coordinated with a shoulder or tote bag for a matching school set. Use waterproof lining to protect your pencil case from those inevitable pen leaks.

DIFFICULTY RATING ✷✷

FINISHED MEASUREMENTS

9 x 7½in (23 x 19cm)

MATERIALS

½yd (50cm) main fabric

Small amount of plain fabric for front band

½yd (50cm) waterproof lining fabric

½yd (50cm) fusible fleece

7in (18cm) zipper

Matching sewing thread

CUTTING GUIDE

Front: 10¼ x 6¼in (26 x 16cm), cut 1 x main fabric, 1 x lining, 1 x fusible fleece

Front band: 10½ x 3¾in (26½ x 9½cm), cut 1 x plain fabric, 1 x lining, 1 x fusible fleece

Back: 10¼ x 8¾in (26 x 22cm), cut 1 x main fabric, 1 x lining, 1 x fusible fleece

NOTES

All seam allowances are ⅜in (1cm) unless otherwise stated

1 Cut out the pattern pieces following the cutting guide. Fuse one piece of fusible fleece to the wrong side of each outer piece.

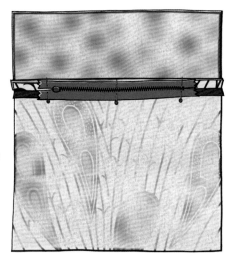

2 Machine baste (tack) the main outer front and plain front band pieces with right sides together, using a long stitch length. Press the seam open. With the wrong side facing up (fusible fleece side up), place the zipper face down on the seam, centered on the width and with the teeth aligned with the seam join. Pin the zipper in place at the top and bottom stops.

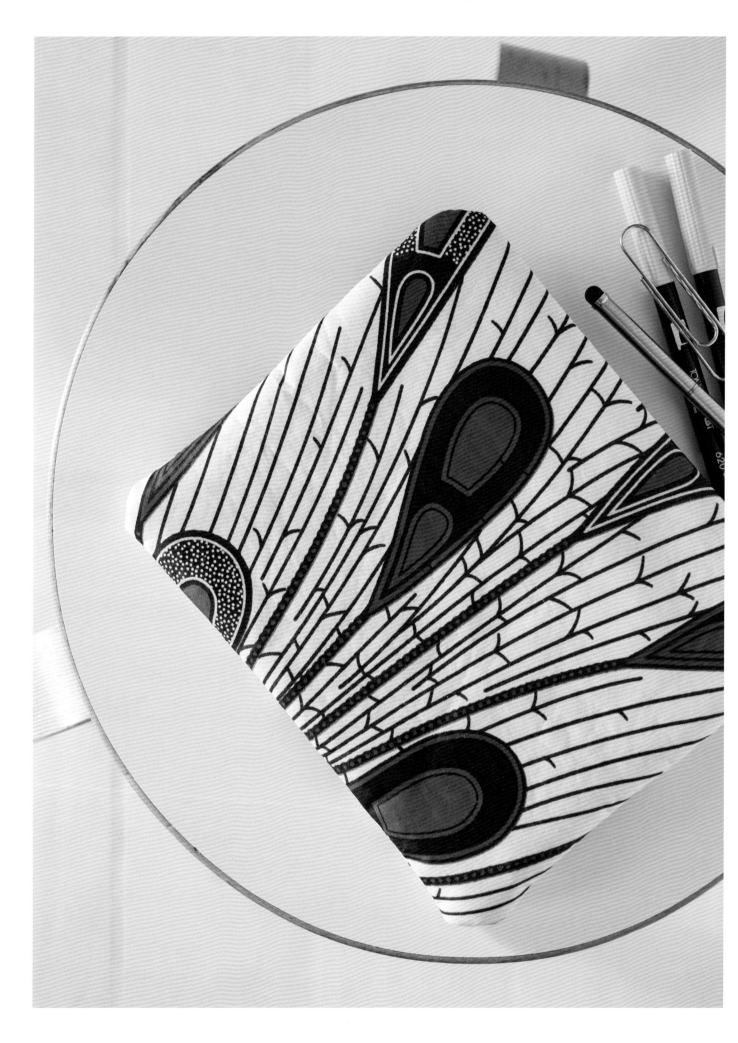

3 Stitch the zipper in place from the right side, keeping the zipper open a little, and stitching around both the long and short sides, close to the teeth. Once you have attached your zipper, carefully unpick the long stitches (from the right side) on the seam to reveal your zipper teeth.

4 With right sides together, stitch the completed front outer to the back of the outer case on all sides. Press and trim the seam, trimming the corners. Keep wrong side out.

5 To make the lining, stitch the larger front lining piece to the front band lining piece with right sides together, leaving an 8in (20cm) gap centered on the seam to match the zippered opening on the outer case. Press the seam. Then stitch the back lining to the front lining on all sides, leaving an 8in (20cm) gap in the bottom edge. Press the seams and trim the corners.

6 With both cases wrong side out, insert the outer case into the lining case through the matching gap in the seam. Line up the seams in the opening so that the zipper is centered. Ensure that the zipper is half open.

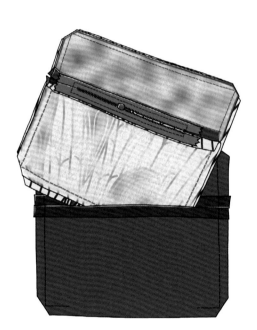

7 With the seam allowance turned under, slip stitch the opening in the lining to the outer edge of the zipper tape on both sides of the gap.

8 Open the zipper fully and turn the pencil case through the gap in the bottom of the lining so that the case is right side out. Slip stitch the gap in the lining closed then push the lining back into the corners. Fill with your favorite pens and close the zipper.

SOPHIA SHOULDER BAG

This boxy shoulder bag makes for the perfect accessory. It is large enough to carry all your essentials, yet compact and stylish, and the contrasting satin lining elevates this make and adds a touch of the "wow" factor. Take care when positioning motifs or patterns so that when cutting out, you make the most of the fabric.

DIFFICULTY RATING ✱✱

FINISHED MEASUREMENTS

Bag: 10½ x 9 x 3in (27 x 23 x 8cm)

Handles: 34 x 4in (86½ x 10cm)

MATERIALS

1yd (1m) outer fabric

1yd (1m) lining fabric

1yd (1m) fusible fleece

Matching sewing thread

CUTTING GUIDE

Cut the following in each of outer fabric, lining fabric, and fusible fleece:

Front: 12 x 10in (30 x 25cm)

Back: 12 x 10in (30 x 25cm)

Flap: 12 x 10in (30 x 25cm)

Side gusset x 2: 10 x 4in (25 x 10cm)

Base gusset: 12 x 4in (30 x 10cm)

Cut the following in the outer fabric and fusible fleece:

Shoulder strap: 35½ x 4in (90 x 10cm)

NOTES

All seam allowances are ⅜in (1cm) unless otherwise stated

1 Cut the pattern pieces following the cutting guide from the outer, lining, and fusible fleece. Fuse the fleece to the wrong side of the front, back, flap, side gussets and base gusset outer fabric pieces of the bag.

3 With right sides facing, stitch the front outer piece to the side gussets along the long edge and repeat to stitch the gusset to the back outer piece. Press both seams. Your "box" bag is beginning to take shape.

2 Pin, baste (tack), and stitch the front outer piece to the base piece with right sides together, along the longer edge. Repeat to stitch the back outer piece to the opposite long edge of the base piece. Press both seams.

4 To complete the base, stitch the short open side gusset to the base to close the seam. Do this on both sides. Press and then trim the seams.

5 Keep the bag wrong side out. Pin and baste (tack) the outer flap piece and the lining for the flap piece right sides together. Sew around the two long sides and one short side, and then turn the piece inside out so that the right sides are on the outside. Center the flap on the inside raw edge at the top of the bag, positioning it with the right sides of the main fabric together, and raw edges aligned. Pin and stitch in place. Press and trim the seam.

6 To make the handle, fold the handle strip in half lengthwise, with wrong sides together. Press. As if you were making bias binding, open out to reveal the crease along the middle. Fold each long edge toward the center. Press. Fold again so that the folds meet right sides together, then topstitch ¼in (6mm) along both long edges. Your strap is now ready to be attached to the bag.

7 With the bag wrong side out, slip the handle inside the bag, and center it on the side gusset at each end, with raw edges aligned. Pin and stitch in place taking a ¼in (6mm) seam allowance, and checking that the handle isn't twisted.

8 Repeat steps 2–4 to make a "box" shape in the lining fabric, but leave a 4in (10cm) gap in one of the long edges of the base seam where it is stitched to either the front or back piece. You will use this gap to turn the bag through to the right side when complete.

9 Turn the outer bag right side out and, with the lining bag wrong side out, insert the outer bag into the lining so that the right sides are facing. Ensure that the handle is out of the way inside the bag between the outer and lining. Pin, baste, and stitch the outer and lining together at the top. Trim the seam.

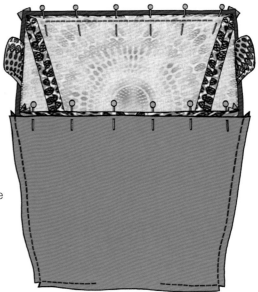

10 Carefully pull the outer bag through the gap in the lining to the right side. Slip stitch the gap closed and push the lining back into the outer bag.

11 Topstitch the top edge of the bag ¼in (6mm) from the edge, keeping the handles away from the bag as you stitch. For a really smart finish you can also topstitch the bag flap on the sides and lower edge.

MARILYN MAKE-UP BAG

This make-up bag is an essential accessory. Perfect either for use at home or for when traveling, it is lined with a waterproof fabric to protect the inside of the bag.

DIFFICULTY RATING ✳✳

FINISHED MEASUREMENTS

10½ x 6 x 6½in (27 x 15 x 17cm)

MATERIALS

½yd (½m) outer fabric

½yd (½m) waterproof lining fabric

½yd (½m) lightweight iron-on interfacing

½yd (½m) fusible fleece

12in (30cm) zipper

Matching sewing thread

Sewing clips

CUTTING GUIDE

Cut 2 of the following in each of the outer fabric, waterproof lining fabric, and fusible fleece, and interfacing:

Base

Side

NOTES

All seam allowances are ⅜in (1cm) unless otherwise stated

TEMPLATES REQUIRED

Base

Side

1 Copy the templates on page 124 on to paper, pin the paper patterns to the fabric, and cut out the pattern pieces following the Cutting Guide. Fuse one piece of interfacing and one piece of fleece to the wrong side of each of the outer fabric pieces (sides and bases).

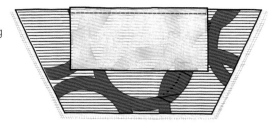

2 With right sides facing, center one outer base piece on one of the outer bag pieces along the longer edge. Pin and stitch together. Repeat to attach the other side and base pieces together and press the seams open. Do the same to sew the lining pieces together.

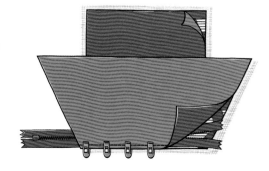

3 Lay one side of the outer bag flat with the right side facing you. Open the zipper and place it right side down on the top edge, then place the lining piece on top with the right side down. Align all the raw edges, and use sewing clips to hold the layers together as you sew. Stitch all three layers together with the zipper sandwiched in between.

4 Close the zipper to make sure it doesn't catch, then open it again, take the lining and outer pieces to one side with wrong sides facing and repeat step 3 to attach the remaining outer and lining pieces to the other side of the zipper. Trim down the interfacing along the zipper, taking care not to cut into the stitching line.

5 Fold back the attached fabric pairs so that the zipper is in the middle, with the outer fabric facing up and the lining underneath. Press the fabric next to the zipper and then topstitch along both sides of the zipper using matching thread.

6 To complete the make-up bag, fold the outer pieces to one side so they are together with right sides facing, and repeat with the lining pieces to the other side. Open the zipper about halfway. Stitch all around the edge of the bag, leaving a 5in (12cm) gap in the base of the lining to turn the bag through. In both the outer and lining base pieces, leave the short ends unstitched, only stitching the long edge. Trim down the interfacing and fleece on the seams.

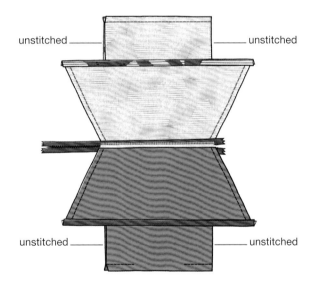

unstitched — unstitched

unstitched — unstitched

7 To create the bag's rounded base, open one short end in the outer base and open the matching short end in the lining, with the seams running down the center. Pin together around their edges; they will form a triangular pointed shape. Stitch together. Repeat for the other end in the outer base and lining. Trim back the fleece layer along the seam allowance.

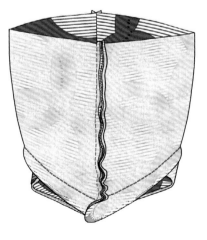

8 To finish the bag, pull the outer bag through the gap in the lining and the zipper so that it is right side out. Slip stitch the gap in the lining closed and then push the lining back inside the outer bag. Close the zipper to reveal the completed shape.

TONI BOX BAG

The fleece lining gives this generous tote bag a comfortable yet sturdy feel. Use a bold fabric to make it into a statement piece, or really make it your own by using contrasting fabrics for the side panels— faux leather is a favorite of mine, or try other heavyweight fabrics, such as denim.

DIFFICULTY RATING ✱✱

FINISHED SIZE

Bag: 4 x 17½ x 6¾in (35 x 44 x 17cm)

Handles: 27in (68cm)

MATERIALS

1½yd (1.5m) outer fabric, 45in (112cm) wide

1½yd (1.5m) fusible fleece

1½yd (1.5m) lightweight iron-on interfacing

1½yd (1.5m) lining fabric, 45in (112cm) wide

1 x metal no-sew snap closure

Matching sewing thread

CUTTING GUIDE

Cut 2 of each of the following in main fabric and fusible fleece:

Front/back: 17¼ x 13½in (44 x 34cm)

Sides: 13½ x 8½in (34 x 21.5cm)

Facing: 3 x 21in (7.5 x 53.5cm)

Cut 2 of each of the following in lining and interfacing:

Front/back: 15 x 12½in (38 x 32cm)

Sides lining: 11½ x 7½in (29 x 19cm)

Cut 2 in each of the main fabric and interfacing:

Handles: 4 x 28in (10 x 71cm)

NOTES

All seam allowances are ⅜in (1cm) unless otherwise stated

1 Fuse the fleece to the wrong side of the outer bag fabric pieces. Fuse the interfacing on the wrong side of the lining fabric (see page 112). Keep any spare fusible fleece to reinforce the snap closure.

2 To make the handles, fold the handle strip in half lengthwise, with wrong sides together. Press. As if you were making bias binding, open out to reveal the crease along the middle. Fold each long edge toward the center crease. Press. Fold again so that the folds meet right sides together, then topstitch ⅛in (3mm) from both edges or use an edge foot. Repeat for the second handle and then put the handles to one side.

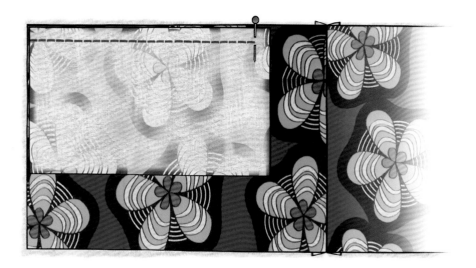

3 Stitch the outer front and back together with right sides facing at the short end. Press the seam open. Pin one side panel piece to the front/back pieces starting at the top left side. Line up raw edges and sew with right sides facing. Stop stitching ½in (1.3cm) before the end of this seam—mark the point with a pin.

4 Repeat to attach the second side piece to the opposite edge, remembering to stop stitching ½in (1.3cm) before the end of the seam. Stitch the back piece to the attached side panels in the same way. Your box is beginning to take shape. Trim the bulk interfacing along the seams, taking care not to cut into the stitching lines as you do so.

5 Stand the bag on the base with the base seam centered. Now stitch the base of the bag closed by sewing the bottom short end of the side panel to one end of the base, stitch with right sides together. Repeat to attach the other side panel. The box shape is now complete.

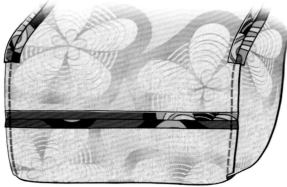

6 Turn the bag right side out to attach the handles. Position the handles approximately 3in (7.5cm) in from the side seam on the right side. Line up the raw edges and pin in place at both ends of the front and back, taking care not to twist the handles.

7 Now mark the center on the wrong side of both facing pieces for the position of the snap closures. Take your time to make sure you position your mark accurately as you will use this as a guide to insert both sides of the snap closure. Then, stitch the two pieces of facing together right side to right side at the short ends to make a circle.

8 To construct the facing, stitch the facing strips right sides together at the short ends to create a circle. With bag still right side out, turn the facing wrong side out and slip it over the top of the bag so that the pieces are right sides together, ling up the raw edges. Pin or clip in place, then stitch. Press and trim the seam.

9 Pull the facing upward and understitch the facing only to the seam allowance ¼in (6mm) from the bag/facing seam. Turn the facing to the inside and topstitch in place, taking care to keep the handles out of the way, use ¼in (6mm) foot to stitch ¼in (6mm) from the top seam where the bag joins the facing. This will give your bag a neat, professional finish.

10 Repeat steps 3–5 to sew the lining in exactly the same way, but leaving a 9in (23cm) gap in the base seam when you sew the lining front and back pieces together.

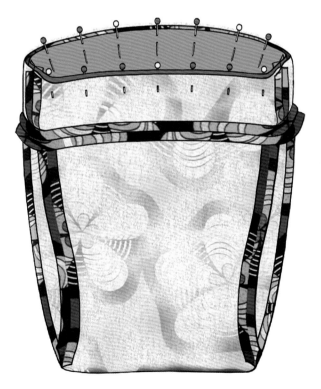

11 Turn the outer bag wrong side out, with the lining right side out insert the lining into the outer bag. Stand the facing up and line the raw edge of the lining with the raw edge of the facing, right sides together, pin and stitch.

12 Carefully turn the outer fabric to the right side through the gap in the bottom of the lining. Then use a matching thread to slip stitch the gap in the lining closed.

SARA SCRUNCHIE

A super-simple project that also makes the perfect gift! This is the ideal make for using up those leftovers from your stash, matching your scrunchie to a skirt, pinafore, or jumpsuit that you've already made in your favorite African wax print fabric.

DIFFICULTY RATING ∗

FINISHED MEASUREMENTS
Length: 10in (25½cm)

Width: ⅜in (1cm)

MATERIALS
Main fabric, 22 x 3½in (56 x 9cm)

9in (23cm) piece of elastic, ⅜in (1cm) wide

Matching sewing thread

Safety pin

NOTES
All seam allowances are ⅜in (1cm) unless otherwise stated

1 Fold the fabric strip in half lengthwise, with right sides facing, and pin. Fold one short end over to the wrong side by ½in (1.3cm).

2 Stitch the long edge, taking care not to sew the folded short end closed—stitch up to the fold line. Center the seam on the width and press the seam open.

3 Turn the strip to the right side through one of the open ends. Attach a safety pin to one end of the elastic and thread it through the strip, holding the other end and gathering the fabric as you go.

4 Pull both ends of the elastic out, overlap the ends, and zig-zag stitch the ends together to secure them.

5 Tuck the raw short end of the scrunchie into the folded end. Slip stitch the folded end to close the join.

IRIS INFINITY SCARF

Infinity scarves are great for when the cooler weather starts setting in. This one is lined with fleece but you can use satin or cotton for a more lightweight accessory. Simple yet stylish, this infinity scarf is long enough to wrap around your neck twice!

DIFFICULTY RATING *

SIZE
One size fits all

FINISHED MEASUREMENTS
Length: 57in (145cm)

Width: 9in (23cm)

MATERIALS
1yd (1m) outer fabric

1yd (1m) fleece or lining fabric of your choice

Matching sewing thread

NOTES
All seam allowances are ⅜in (1cm) unless otherwise stated

1 Pre-wash and "press" your fabric before cutting and sewing (see page 8). Cut two pieces of main fabric 30 x 10½in (74 x 27cm), and two pieces of fleece to the same size.

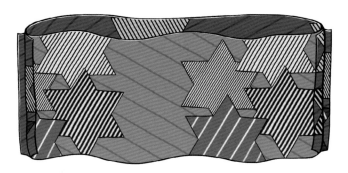

2 With right sides facing, sew both pieces of outer fabric to each other at the shorter ends. Repeat with the fleece or lining fabric. You will now have one circular piece of main fabric and one circular piece of fleece or lining. Press the seams open.

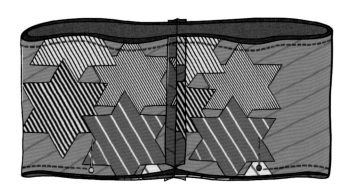

3 With the outer piece wrong side out, slip the fleece or lining fabric piece inside the outer, so that their right sides are together. Pin, baste (tack), and stitch one long edge of the main fabric to the lining. Repeat for the other edge, leaving a 7in (18cm) gap centered on one of the side seams (3½in [9 cm] on either side of the seam).

4 Trim the seam allowance to ¼in (6mm) to reduce the bulk. Press the seams open and reach through the gap to turn the infinity scarf right side out. Slip stitch the gap closed.

EVELYN EYE MASK

Sleep masks are perfect for blocking out distracting light, allowing you to rest and relax. This is another great pattern for using up any odd scraps in your fabric basket.

DIFFICULTY RATING ✱

SIZE

One size fits all

FINISHED MEASUREMENTS

Width: 8in (20cm)

Height: 3½in (9cm)

MATERIALS

Fat quarter of fabric

¼yd (25cm) batting (wadding)

⅔yd (62cm) bias binding, 1¼in (3cm) wide (see page 120 for how to make your own bias binding)

16½in (42cm) ribbon, ⅝in (1.5cm) wide

Matching sewing thread

NOTES

All seam allowances are ⅜in (1cm) unless otherwise stated

CUTTING GUIDE

2 x mask in main fabric

1 x mask in batting

TEMPLATES REQUIRED

Mask

1 Trace the template on page 126 on to paper and cut out a paper pattern. Cut two pieces in the main fabric and one piece from the batting (wadding). Transfer the markings for the ribbon holes onto the fabric.

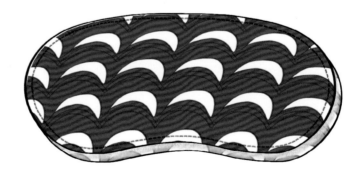

2 Sandwich the batting between the two pieces of main fabric, with the main fabric pieces both right side out. Pin then sew the three layers together taking a ¼in (6mm) seam.

3 Cut the length of ribbon in half and pin each piece in place at each end on what will be the underside of the mask, positioned with the raw edge of the ribbon on the stitched line and the length of ribbon facing inward. Stitch over the existing stitch line to hold the ends of the ribbon in place securely.

4. To attach the binding, start at the center on the lower, shaped edge, overlap the ends and turn them under by ⅜in (1cm). Pin the opened out binding in place and stitch following the instructions on page 121, securing the ribbon in place as you stitch.

5 Before turning the binding to the other side, trim the raw edge of the mask between the two lines of stitching—don't trim the ribbon! Fold the bias binding over to cover the raw edge and topstitch in place from the right side.

MAYA APRON

Aprons always make me think of Bree from "Desperate Housewives" and her perfect "bakes." This apron is a super-simple sew that will add a lot of fun to mealtimes. The patch pockets are useful for keeping all your essentials to hand.

SIZES
small/medium/large

FINISHED MEASUREMENTS
Length: 31½in (80cm)

MATERIALS
2yd (1.8m) fabric, 45in (112cm) wide or 1⅛yd (1m) fabric, 60in (152 cm) wide

Carbon paper

Fusible adhesive (optional)

Matching sewing thread

NOTES
Cut the pattern pieces on the fold.

All seam allowances are ⅜in (1cm) unless otherwise statedw

PATTERN PIECES REQUIRED
Apron
Ties
Strap
Patch pocket

1 Pre-wash and "press" your fabric before cutting and sewing (see page 8). Cut out the pattern pieces. Trace the patch pocket marked positions onto the right side of the front using carbon paper, but do not trace the top line of the pocket. Make two patch pockets following the instructions on page 116.

2 Position the patch pockets using the placement lines on the right side of the main apron piece. Use pins or thin strips of fusible adhesive at the bottom edge and side edges of the pocket to temporarily fix the pockets in place while sewing. Keep the adhesive strip within the ¼in (6mm) seam allowance. Topstitch in place from the right side. Remove the adhesive strips if using.

3 Finish all the raw edges on the top, sides, and hem of the main apron piece. To do this, turn the edge to the wrong side by ⅜in (1cm). Press. Turn under again by ⅜in (1cm) and press. Pin in place, folding any corners over neatly, and top stitch ¼in (6mm) from the edge from the right side.

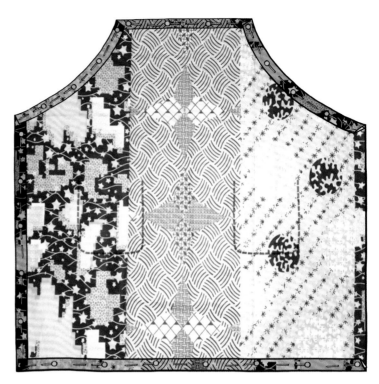

4 To make the ties and neck strap, fold each strip in half lengthwise, with wrong sides together. Press. As if you were making bias binding (see page 120), open out to reveal the crease along the middle. Fold each long edge toward the center crease. Press. Fold again so that the folds meet right sides together, then topstitch along all long edges and short ends, ⅛in (3mm) from the edge. Repeat for each piece.

5 To attach the neck strap, pin it in position on the wrong side of the main apron piece at both ends, making sure the strap isn't twisted. Position it 1in (2.5cm) down from top edge of the bib and pin in place. Topstitch from the right sides, sewing a box shape and with an "X" in the center to secure it in place.

6 Position one end of each waist tie 1in (2.5cm) in from the side edges at the waist. Pin in place then topstitch a box with an "X" in the center from the right side to secure.

HARRIET HAIR TIE

This on-trend accessory is an ideal quick make—perfect as a gift. Small scale fabrics are ideal, or match the main or contrasting fabric in one of your favorite African wax print garments.

DIFFICULTY RATING ✱

FINISHED MEASUREMENTS
33½ x 2½in (85 x 6cm)

MATERIALS
1yd (1m) fabric

1yd (1m) craft wire

Wire cutters

Matching sewing thread

CUTTING GUIDE
2 x Hair tie in main fabric

NOTES
All seam allowances are ⅜in (1cm) unless otherwise stated

TEMPLATE REQUIRED
Hair tie

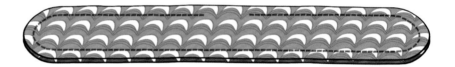

1 Trace the template on page125 onto paper and cut out the paper pattern. Cut two pieces in the main fabric. Stitch both pieces together with right sides facing, leaving a 4in (10cm) gap on one of the long edges.

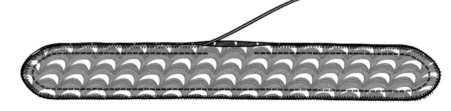

2 Insert the length of craft wire into the ditch of the seam allowance. Stitch the raw edges together using zig-zag stitch, enclosing the wire between the seam and the zig-zag stitches. Start and stop stitching either side of the gap. Trim the end of the wire with wire cutters or sturdy scissors (not your dressmaking scissors!).

3 Turn the hair tie right side out through the gap and slip stitch the gap closed. Press. Position the tie with the gap in the wiring at the back, then twist the ends together to hold in place.

HATTIE HEADBAND

A lovely little accessory and perfect for styling your hair while keeping it off your face when at the gym or in a yoga class — why not make a matching boxy shoulder bag for your kit (see page 86)? This is a great stashbuster, too.

DIFFICULTY RATING ✱

FINISHED MEASUREMENTS
One size

MATERIALS
Fat quarter of fabric

7in (18cm) elastic, 1in (2.5cm) wide

Matching sewing thread

CUTTING GUIDE
Cut the following pieces from the fabric:

10 x 3in (25.5 x 7.5cm) strip

17 x 7in (43 x 18cm) strip

NOTES
All seam allowances are ⅜in (1cm) unless otherwise stated

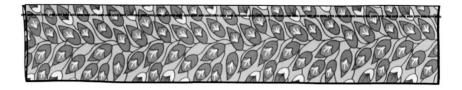

1 Sew the smaller piece together along the long edges, with right sides facing, taking a ¼in (6mm) seam allowance. Press the seam open down the center. Repeat with the larger piece, using a ½in (1.3cm) seam. Turn both pieces right sides out and press with the seam centered down the middle.

2 Attach a safety pin to one end of the elastic and thread it through the channel in the smaller piece, keeping hold of the other end as you gather the fabric. Pin the elastic in place at both raw ends and zig-zag stitch to secure it in place.

3 Prepare the larger piece. With the seam facing down, use a pin to mark the center of one end of the strip. Fold both sides in toward the center pin to create a small pleat (see page 110). Press and pin to hold in place. Repeat with the other end.

4 Place the larger piece with the seam face down. Position the smaller, elasticated strip on top, with the seam facing up. Match the raw edges at the ends and stitch together using a ⅜in (1cm) seam allowance. Press the seam allowance then turn the headband over to the right side and it's ready to wear.

FREDERICA FACE MASK

While it wasn't on anyone's wish-list in 2019, the humble facemask has been catapulted into the category of essential fashion item! Make one up as a matching accessory and remember: "don't touch your face!" They are a great way to use up scrap fabric, and a super-quick and easy sew.

DIFFICULTY RATING: *

FINISHED MEASUREMENTS
Width: 8in (20cm)
Height: 4½in (10 cm)

MATERIALS
Fat quarter (approx. 18 x 24in/ 45 x 60 cm) of fabric

17in (44cm) shirring or narrow band elastic

Matching sewing thread

CUTTING GUIDE
Cut 2 x template in main fabric.

NOTE
All seam allowances are ⅜in (1cm) unless otherwise stated.

TEMPLATE REQUIRED
Face mask

1 Trace the template on page 123 on to paper and cut out the pattern. Fold the fabric in two with right sides facing, and pin the paper pattern to fabric. Transfer the dart markings to the wrong side of the fabric (see page 109). Cut out two fabric pieces, then press the fold line of each dart in place.

2 To sew darts closed, start at the raw edge and stitch toward the point of the dart. Do not backstitch at the point, but leave long thread ends and tie a double knot to close the stitching line. Cut the ends of the thread and press the darts to one side from the wrong side.

3 Place the two face mask pieces right sides together, lining up the dart stitching lines and the raw edges. Stitch around the raw edges leaving one short straight side unstitched. Clip the seam allowance on the curved edges, then turn your face mask through to the right side at the unstitched end, and press.

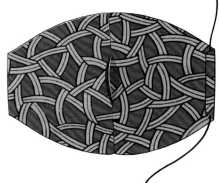

4 Cut two pieces of elastic each approximately 8½in (22cm) long. Fold over the unstitched raw edge of the face mask by ¼in (6mm) followed by another ¼in (6mm). Center one piece of elastic inside the fold and pin in place.

5 Machine-sew over the elastic using a zigzag stitch. Remember to backstitch at the beginning and end of each seam.

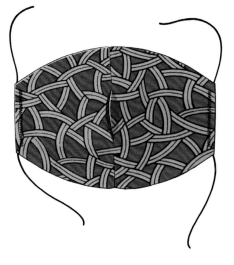

6 At the other short end, fold over ¼in (6mm) of fabric. Center the other piece of elastic inside the fold, pin in place, and continue as in step 5.

7 On each side, tie the ends of the elastic together and you're good to go.

TECHNIQUES

WORKING WITH PATTERNS AND TEMPLATES

The garment patterns on the pull-out sheets at the back of this book are printed to their actual size. You will need to trace them from the sheets onto tracing paper, greaseproof paper, or pattern paper, which is available from sewing and haberdashery stores. (Whatever you use, check that it is thin enough to see through.) Trace the pieces in the size that you need (the key on each pattern sheet shows you which line to follow) and cut them out.

On pages 123–126 you will find templates for some of the smaller accessories. Simply photocopy the templates, enlarging them if necessary (indicated on the template). Pin the photocopied template to your fabric (drawing around it if you wish), and then cut around it (or along the drawn line). If the template has markings, transfer them using a water-soluble marker, dressmaker's pencil or pins.

POSITIONING PATTERN PIECES ON THE FABRIC

In dressmaking, the vast majority of pattern pieces need to be cut from a double layer of fabric. You generally have to fold your fabric in a particular way before you pin the pattern pieces to it and cut them out. There are three main ways of folding the fabric (see right).

Many pattern pieces are symmetrical—the front of a bodice or the back of a shirt, for example. Instead of being cut as one huge paper pattern, these pieces are often cut out as a half piece and the center line is placed on the fold of the fabric. A double-headed arrow on a pattern indicates an edge that has to be placed on the fold.

Sometimes you may have two pieces that are the same shape but need to be mirror images of each other—the left and right sides of a shirt front, for example, or left and right sleeves. If you're cutting these from a doubled layer of fabric, there's no problem—the two pieces will automatically be mirror images when they're cut out. But if you're cutting them from a single layer of fabric, you must remember to flip the pattern over before you cut out the second piece so that you get a left- and a right-hand piece.

Fold the fabric, then pin the pattern pieces in place and either draw around them with tailor's chalk and cut out, or simply cut around the pattern pieces. Lay out all the pattern pieces on your fabric before you begin cutting to make sure you're using the most economical layout and avoid wasting fabric. If you're using a print and want to match the pattern across two adjoining pieces, you may also find that you need to move the pieces around slightly to get the best result.

Fold in half widthwise, matching up the selvages.

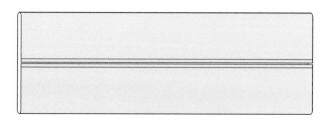

Fold both selvages in to meet the center.

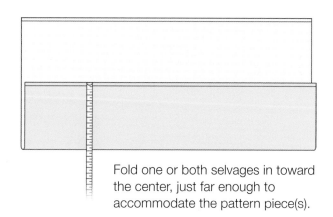

Fold one or both selvages in toward the center, just far enough to accommodate the pattern piece(s).

PATTERN MATCHING

Often in dressmaking you are advised to follow the straight grain when cutting out your pattern pieces in your fabric. However, with African wax print fabrics you should follow the design. This will mean cutting on either the straight grain or the cross grain, depending on the most pleasing direction of the print. For more information on pattern matching African wax print fabrics, see pages 10–11.

Pattern matching by eye takes time and experience. Play around with the paper pattern pieces and your fabric, while at the same time trying to picture how the finished garment will look. Take your time—pattern placement often takes longer than the actual sewing but once cut, and the pattern placement is correct, the sewing can be straightforward. The methods below can help when pattern matching with non-directional or detailed designs and will depend on whether you are cutting out from a single layer or double (on the fold).

TRACING AND CUTTING THE DESIGN

1 Cut out a copy of the pattern piece in pattern paper.

2 Lay your fabric out flat in a single layer. Place the copied pattern paper over key pieces, such as center fronts or backs, and cut out one piece.

3 With the paper pattern still attached, trace the outline of the main elements of the fabric design with a soft pencil.

4 Match the tracing to the fabric pattern to cut out a matching second piece, remembering to flip the pattern if you need a mirrored piece. Match seamlines.

CUTTING DOUBLE

1 Fold your fabric in half and match the selvages, checking that the pattern is matched along the edges.

2 Place the paper pattern aligned with an element of the design, using pins through the two layers at key elements of the design. Lift the edge to check that the pin marks the same design underneath.

3 Pin the fabric edges so that they won't move, and cut out the two layers on the fold.

PATTERN MARKS FOR CUTTING OUT

GRAIN LINES

These lines indicate where the grain line (or direction of the fabric) should be when that pattern piece is cut out in fabric. These marks don't need to be transferred onto your fabric; however, you do need to pay attention to them as they tell you how to position the pattern piece in relation to the straight grain in your fabric (but see also Pattern Matching, left).

PLACE TO FOLD LINE

When the grain line turns in at each end at right angles, it means that the edge of the pattern that the arrows point to needs to be placed on a lengthwise fold in the fabric. You cut around all other sides of the pattern except this one on the fold and you will end up with one big symmetrical fabric piece once the pattern is cut out.

EXTENSION LINES

Some bigger pattern pieces have been printed in two parts, as they are too big to fit onto the pattern sheets in one piece. Where this is the case, you will see a broken "extension" line with scissors at each end, where one part of a piece ends, and a corresponding extension line on the other part of the piece. Trace the first part of the piece to the extension line, then align it with the extension line of the second part of the same piece and trace that to complete the pattern piece.

ALTERATION LINES

Double parallel lines show you where to lengthen or shorten a pattern piece.

TRANSFERRING PATTERN MARKS TO THE FABRIC

Patterns are also marked to show where to position features like pockets, buttonholes, and other fastenings, or where you need to place darts or pleats. Transfer any markings to the fabric before you unpin the pattern pieces. You can do this with either a chalk pencil, carbon paper, or tailor's tacks (see page 113), or by using scissors to make notches in the fabric. If your fabric is folded, push a pin straight down through the fabric at the marked point, and then mark the position on the bottom layer of fabric.

Notches are found on the edge of patterns on seam lines, and are used to help you match up seams and join the correct pieces together.

DRESSMAKING TECHNIQUES

DARTS

A dart is a tapered fold in a piece of fabric, which is stitched to give a garment shape. Darts are principally used on women's garments to shape the fabric around the bust, hips, and waist.

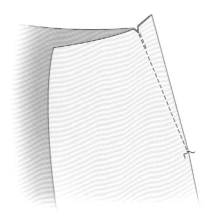 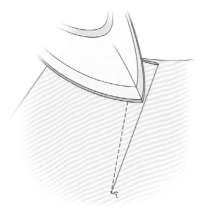

1 With right sides together and matching notches, fold through the middle of the dart. Sew a straight line from the matched notches to the point. Do not back stitch at the point.

2 Lay the fabric with the dart flat to one side and press to the point only, but no further. Then press it down toward the hem. Do this from the wrong side first and then press from the right side. Use a tailor's ham if you have one. Remove the tailor's tack.

PLEATS

Pleats are vertical folds that are usually formed by doubling fabric back on itself and securing it in place.

INVERTED BOX PLEATS AND BOX PLEATS

Inverted box pleats are used in the Priscilla T-shirt on page 22 and the Diana T-shirt Tunic on page 25. Inverted box pleats have two fold lines that meet at a common placement line; the back folds face away from each other. Box pleats have two fold lines and two placement lines. The front folds face away from each other and the back folds face toward each other.

Box pleats

Inverted box pleats

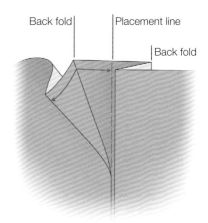

FORMING INVERTED BOX PLEATS

Both inverted and box pleats are formed on the right side of the fabric using exactly the same process; the only difference between them is in the direction of the fold lines to the placement line. The diagrams below illustrate how to form a single inverted pleat.

 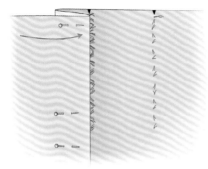

1 To transfer the pleat markings, use doubled thread to work a row of large, uneven basting (tacking) stitches through the pattern to the right side of the fabric. Cut the thread at the center of each long stitch and carefully remove the pattern, avoiding pulling the threads. Alternatively, use tailor's chalk or a fabric marker pen to mark the position of the pleat on the wrong side of the fabric, using pins to mark the fold lines and placement line to guide you when forming the pleat from the right side.

2 Working from the right side, fold the fabric along a fold line, then bring the fold to its placement line. Pin the pleat in place through all the layers. Repeat with the second fold line, bringing it over to meet at the placement line, and remove all the thread markings as you pin. Press the pleats in place before basting in position close to each fold line, stitching through all the layers of fabric and removing the pins as you go.

TIP

For the Priscilla T-shirt and Diana T-shirt Tunic projects you can widen the gap between the pleat lines directly onto the fabric or alter the pattern as you prefer, in order to increase the size of the pleats and, consequently, to make the neckline smaller or larger as required.

ADDING FULLNESS TO SLEEVES

The sleeve used in the Betsy Dress on page 62, is a "hack" of the Mary Shirt sleeve. The sleeve was lengthened, with fullness added at both the top and the bottom of the drafted sleeve. This is done using what is called the "slash and spread" method and is a great addition to your sewing and drafting skills, so that you can either add fullness at the top of the sleeve, the bottom of the sleeve, or both.

1 Retrace the pattern piece for the sleeve. Lay it onto a larger piece of pattern paper and decide how much fullness you would like to add. The fullness should be evenly distributed across the sleeve. Draw lines in the middle of the sleeve and then two or more lines evenly distributed either side of the center (depending on the size of your sleeve).

2 Cut down the lines and separate the sleeve pieces, keeping the broad outline of the sleeve and leaving a gap of ⅜-2in (1-5cm) between each cut piece, depending on the required fullness.

3 Stick the cut pieces onto the larger piece of paper and cut around your adapted sleeve pattern to cut out your new sleeve piece. This method adds fullness at the top and the bottom.

4 To only add fullness at the top, cut ("slash") from the top, down the lines but stop just before the end so as not to cut the lines completely open. Spread the top of the sleeve like a fan, so that fullness is added at the top (evenly distributed). Stick down onto a piece of paper and cut out the new shape.

5 To add fullness at the bottom, repeat step 4 but from the bottom; cut lines from the bottom to the top, stopping just short of cutting the lines fully open, open at the bottom, spread evenly, stick down, and cut out a new piece.

INTERFACING

Interfacing is a special type of fabric applied to the inside of a garment to strengthen specific parts, such as collars, cuffs, and buttonholes. Interfacings come in several weights and degrees of crispness and can be woven or non-woven, sew-in or iron-on. With such a wide range available it is possible to find an interfacing suitable for every type of fabric. If you are unsure which is best for your fabric, ask the salesperson for a recommendation.

APPLYING IRON-ON INTERFACING

Iron-on interfacings are the easiest to use and are the ones that we recommend for the projects in this book. They have heat-sensitive glue on one side; the manufacturer normally provides instructions for your iron heat setting on the ends of the interfacing rolls, but this information may also be printed down the edges of the interfacing itself.

Lay the cut interfacing pieces adhesive side down on the wrong side of the garment pieces. To fix the interfacing in position, set your iron to a steam setting following the manufacturer's instructions., then place the iron firmly on it for a few seconds at a time. Lift the iron and reposition it; do not slide the iron across, as this could move the interfacing and cause creases.

Allow the interfacing to cool. Check that it is fused all over and re-press any loose areas. Continue stitching your garment together as normal.

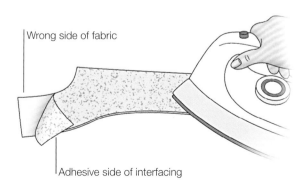

Wrong side of fabric

Adhesive side of interfacing

STITCHES

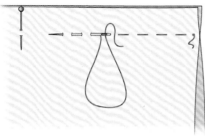

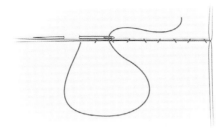

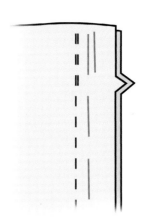

BASTING (TACKING)

Working from right to left, take evenly spaced stitches about ¼in (6 mm) long through the fabric layers, sewing close to the seamline but within the seam allowance. Take several stitches onto your needle at one time, before drawing the thread through the fabric.

SLIP STITCH

This is a handstitch worked to close gaps in seams. Bring the needle out through the seam allowance to hide the knot in the seam. Take the needle across to the other seam, picking up a few threads and emerging approximately ⅛in (3 mm) along. Take the needle back to the opposite side, then repeat, working across the seam and pulling the thread to join the two sides.

BACKSTITCH (MACHINE)

A short length of reverse stitching at the beginning and end of a row of straight stitching, made by using the reverse lever on the sewing machine. This secures the stitches and gives extra strength to the seam.

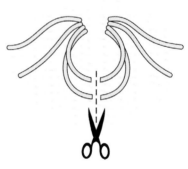

TAILOR'S TACKS

To work a tailor's tack, thread the needle with a double loop of cotton in a contrasting color to your fabric, but do not knot the ends. At the marked point on the pattern, take the needle down through the fabric and back up again to the right side, and then repeat the process through the same stitch to leave a loop on the surface of the fabric. Leave a tail of thread on each side and do not draw the loop tight. When you remove the paper pattern, the tack will remain on the surface of the right side of the fabric as a position guide. If the tailor's tack is worked over two layers of fabric, gently pull the layers apart and cut through the threads of the loop in the center; this will leave the threads of the tack stitching on both pieces of fabric.

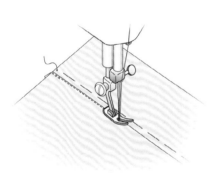

STITCH-IN-THE-DITCH

A row of straight stitching made very close to a seam on the right side, so that it "sinks" into the seam groove. It is used to create a defined edge or to give an invisible finish, for example to hold a facing in place inside a neckline.

TOPSTITCHING

Topstitching is often done to finish an edge—as well as being decorative, it prevents the underside of the edge from rolling to the outside. Working from the right side, line up your finished seam edge on the chosen guideline and begin stitching, turning any corners by lifting your presser foot and pivoting your fabric around the needle. Trim your thread ends even with the raw edges.

ZIPPERS

INSERTING A CENTERED ZIPPER

A centered zipper sits along the center of the opening, with the stitching that holds the zipper in place machined on both sides at an equal distance from the seamline.

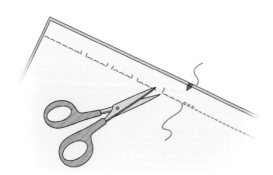

1 Stitch the garment seam up to the zipper notch; reverse stitch to secure. Adjust your machine stitch length to the largest size and machine baste (tack) the zipper opening edges together without reverse stitching at the ends.

Using a sharp pair of small scissors, snip the stitches on the bobbin thread at ⅜in (1cm) intervals along the zipper opening, to allow for easy removal later on. Finish the seam allowances (see page 118) and press the seam open.

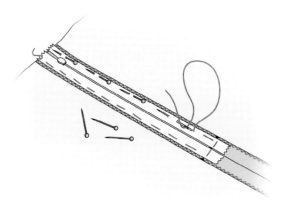

2 Place the zipper face down on the seam allowances, so that the zipper teeth run down the center of the seam and the bottom stop is just below the notch. Pin and hand baste the zipper in place.

3 Working from the right side of the garment, with a regular stitch length on your machine, stitch the zipper in place. To do this, have your zipper foot to the left of the needle; starting just below the zipper stop at the seamline, stitch three or four stitches across the bottom, pivot your work, and stitch up to the top of the zipper, keeping your stitching parallel to the seamline. Reverse stitch at each end of the stitching to secure.

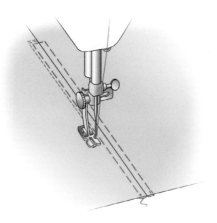

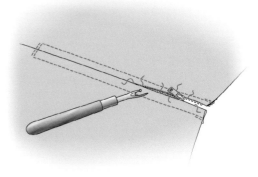

4 Reposition the zipper foot to the right of the needle. Starting again at the base of the zipper, stitch the other side in place, as before. Remove the basting stitches and unpick the seam covering the zipper teeth.

INSERTING AN INVISIBLE ZIPPER

An invisible zipper is a popular choice for dresses, skirts, and jumpsuits. It is applied to an open seam, on the seam allowances only, so no stitching shows on the right side, and is done with the help of a special grooved zipper foot.

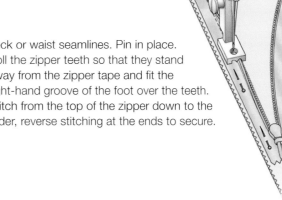

1 Machine baste (tack) the seam where the zipper is to be inserted, using a long stitch length and press the seam open. Unpick the seam from the top to the same length as the zipper teeth. Place the open zipper, right side down, on the right side of the garment, with the zipper teeth running along the seamline and the top stop ⅜in (1cm) down from the neck or waist seamlines. Pin in place. Roll the zipper teeth so that they stand away from the zipper tape and fit the right-hand groove of the foot over the teeth. Stitch from the top of the zipper down to the slider, reverse stitching at the ends to secure.

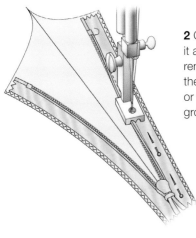

2 Close the zipper to check that it works smoothly then open it again. Pin the other zipper tape to the right side of the remaining garment piece, with the zipper teeth running along the seamline and the top stop ⅜in (1cm) down from the neck or waist seamlines. Fit the zipper teeth into the left-hand groove and stitch in place, as before.

3 Close the zipper and attach a conventional zipper foot to your machine. Pin and baste the garment seam below the zipper, right sides together. Lower the needle down into the fabric at the end of the zipper stitching line, slightly above and to the left; stitch the seam to the lower edge of the garment. Tie the thread ends to secure.

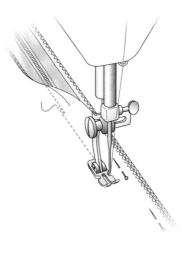

4 To hold the lower zipper ends down, stitch each tape end to the seam allowances only, not the garment.

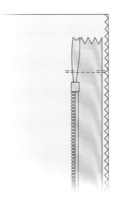

5 Open the zipper and stitch across the top of each tab, keeping the zipper teeth in the rolled-back position for easy sliding. Once the zipper is inserted, remove the basting stitches and sew the center back seam from the hem or the waist to the end of the zipper, to close the seam and the small hole.

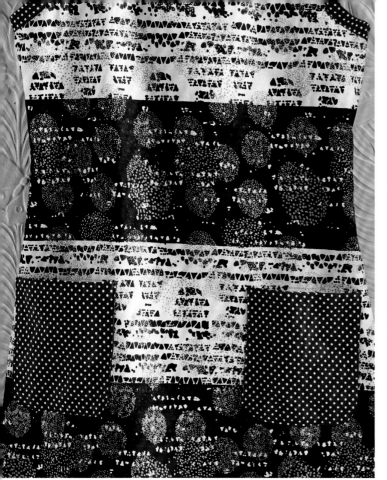

POCKETS

Although there seems to be an endless variety of pocket styles, there are, in fact, only two basic types: patch pockets, which are shaped pieces of fabric that appear on the outside of a garment, adding decoration and styling detail such as those on the Meghan Tunic Dress (page 44); and in-seam pockets, which are placed in the seams. In-seam pockets are used in several projects, including the Althea A-Line Skirt on page 14 and the Diana T-shirt Tunic on page 25. On the pattern sheets, there is one standard pattern for patch pockets and one for in-seam pockets, which can be used in any project that requires them.

PATCH POCKETS

Take care to position patch pockets correctly and make sure they are level. Pockets used in pairs must be the same size and shape.

1 Cut two pocket pieces per pocket. To make one pocket, sew the two pieces together with right sides facing, taking a ¼in (6mm) seam allowance, leaving a 1-2in (2.5-5cm) gap at the bottom.

2 Clip the curves to help create a smooth shape, then turn the pocket through the gap to the right side. Slipstitch the gap closed and press.

3 On the right side of the piece, use the pocket placement lines traced from the pattern to position the pocket pieces. Use strips of fusible web to hold the pattern piece in place while you sew.

IN-SEAM POCKETS

In-seam pockets are concealed in side seams or front panel seams.

1 Cut two pocket pieces per pocket, flipping the pattern if you are cutting through a single layer of fabric only. With right sides facing, pin, baste (tack), and machine stitch each pocket piece to the side seam of the front and back piece, matching any notches and ensuring that the front and back pocket pairs match. Taking the recommended seam allowance, start and stop sewing approximately 1-2in (2.5-5cm) either side of the pocket seam. NOTE: only sew to secure the pocket in place, do not stitch the entire length of the side seam at this stage. Trim the seam allowances if necessary, neaten them together, and turn the pocket to the outside of the seam, then press the seam flat, toward the pocket piece.

2 With right sides together and the raw edges matching, pin, baste, and machine stitch the corresponding garment pieces together in one continuous row of stitching, taking the seam allowance recommended in the project. Decrease the seam allowance slightly around the pockets, pivoting your work at the pocket corners, matching any dots or notches, and reverse stitching at the start and finish to secure. Reinforce the pocket area by working a second row of stitching on top of the first, starting and finishing before and after the corners.

3 Snip into the seam allowance of the back garment at the pocket corners. Neaten the garment seam allowances separately and the pocket seam allowances together, neatening the front and pocket edges in one continuous row of stitching. Press the garment seams open and the whole pocket toward the center front.

FINISHING TECHNIQUES

NEATENING SEAM EDGES

Neatening seam edges prevents them from fraying, helps them lay flat, and gives a tidy, professional touch. There are many ways of doing this, but for a quick effective finish, you can machine overcast the edges using a zigzag stitch.

OPEN SEAM

Zigzag or serge (overlock) on the RS of both single edges of the seam to be joined. With RS together, stitch the seam using the required seam allowance. Press the seam allowances open on the wrong side.

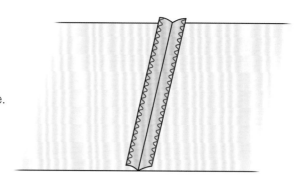

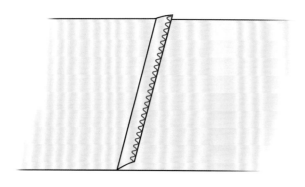

CLOSED SEAM

With right sides together, stitch the seam using the required seam allowance. Zigzag or serge (overlock) the two raw edges together. On the wrong side, press the seam allowance to one side.

DOUBLE-TURNED HEM

Double hemming gives a very neat finish and will prevent fraying.

Following the measurements specified in the project, fold the edge of the fabric over to the wrong side and press. Fold over again, pin, baste (tack), press, and either topstitch (see page 113) in place from the right side or machine stitch from the wrong side, stitching as close as possible to the folded edge.

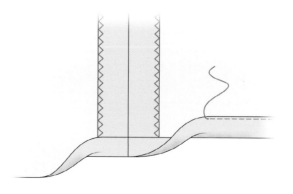

CLIPPING CURVED SEAM ALLOWANCES

This helps curve seams lie flat and will make a real difference to the look of your finished project.

Use the tips of your fabric scissors (don't use tiny embroidery scissors as this will dull the blades) to cut into the seam allowance after stitching, taking great care not to cut through any of the stitches. Seams that curve outward need wedge-shaped notches cut into the seam allowance, while for seams that will curve inward, little slits will do.

TRIMMING CORNERS

For neat corners, you need to trim off the excess fabric across the point before you turn the project right side out, so that the finished corner is neat and square. Cut off the fabric across the corner about 1/8in (3mm) away from the stitching, taking care not to cut through the stitches.

BINDING

Binding is used in several projects in this book. To bind straight edges, strips of fabric cut on the straight of grain can be used. To bind curves (around a neckline, for example), you will need to cut fabric strips on the bias.

MAKING BIAS BINDING

1 Take a square or rectangular piece of fabric, approximately the size of a fat quarter, and press it flat. Fold one corner of the fabric over until the side that is at right angles to the selvage is lined up with the selvage. The resulting fold line is the bias at 45 degrees to the selvage. Using a ruler and chalk, mark lines 2in (5cm) apart, following the 45-degree angle across the fabric.

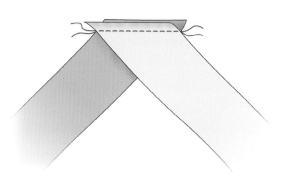

2 Cut along these lines until you have enough strips to make the length you need to go around a hemline, sleeves, or neckline plus approximately 1in (2.5cm). To join strips together, cut the two ends that are to be joined at a 45-degree angle. Place one strip on top of the other, right sides together, and stitch the pieces together diagonally.

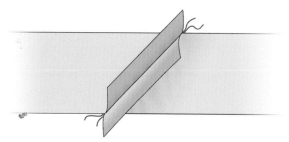

3 Press the seam open and trim the excess from the sides, in line with the edges of the strip. Continue to join the strips together until the bias strip is the length you need for your project.

4 With wrong sides together, fold the strip in half widthwise and press. Open out the central crease, then fold each long edge of the binding in to meet at the central crease and press again.

ATTACHING BIAS BINDING BY MACHINE

You can finish any fabric edge with binding.
Use store-bought or make your own (see opposite),
in either self-fabric or contrasting fabric.

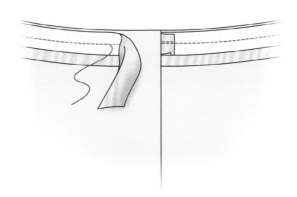

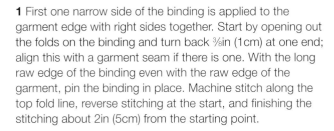

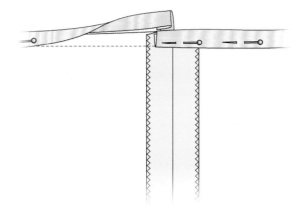

1 First one narrow side of the binding is applied to the garment edge with right sides together. Start by opening out the folds on the binding and turn back ⅜in (1cm) at one end; align this with a garment seam if there is one. With the long raw edge of the binding even with the raw edge of the garment, pin the binding in place. Machine stitch along the top fold line, reverse stitching at the start, and finishing the stitching about 2in (5cm) from the starting point.

2 Trim away the excess binding, leaving ⅜in (1cm) to overlap the turned-back starting end. Still following the top fold line, stitch the remaining binding in place through all layers. Trim the seam to reduce the bulk and press the seam allowances toward the binding. Now flip the opposite folded long edge of the binding over to meet the seamline on the wrong side of the garment, enclosing the raw edge of the garment. Pin in place and then topstitch from the right side.

BUTTONS AND BUTTONHOLES

Many modern sewing machines will stitch buttonholes automatically, but on older machines you may have to stitch them in stages. Check the manual for the correct foot and settings for your machine. Practice sewing your buttonholes first by making the correct length marks and stitching them on a double layer of scrap fabric.

STITCHING A BUTTONHOLE

1 Mark the button positions from the pattern onto the overlapping side using tailor's chalk (right over left for women and girls and left over right for men and boys). Mark your buttonhole either vertically or horizontally, depending on the width of the button band.

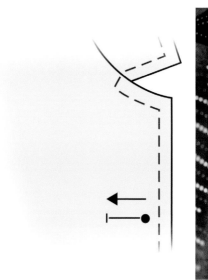

TIP

The position of the buttonholes (either horizontally or vertically) will be determined by the width of the buttonhole band.

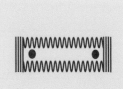

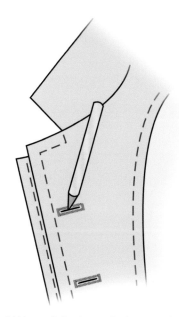

2 Stitch the buttonholes on the right side of the garment; the bar tack ends should lie either side of the marks. Cut between the lines of stitches, snipping inward from each end to ensure accuracy. Pass the button through to ensure that the opening is the correct size.

3 When all the buttonholes are stitched and cut, lay the two front edges right sides together. Mark through each buttonhole, at the end nearest the front edge, onto the underlapping side, to establish the button position. Sew the buttons at the marked positions.

SEWING ON A BUTTON

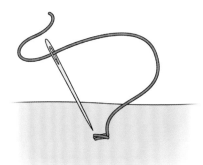

1 Mark the place where you want the button to go. Push the needle up from the back of the fabric and sew a few stitches over and over in this place.

2 Now bring the needle up through one of the holes in the button. Push the needle back down through the second hole and through the fabric. Bring it back up through the first hole. Repeat this five or six times. If there are four holes in the button, use all four of them to make a cross pattern. Make sure that you keep the stitches close together under the middle of the button.

3 Finish with a few small stitches over and over on the back of the fabric and trim the thread.

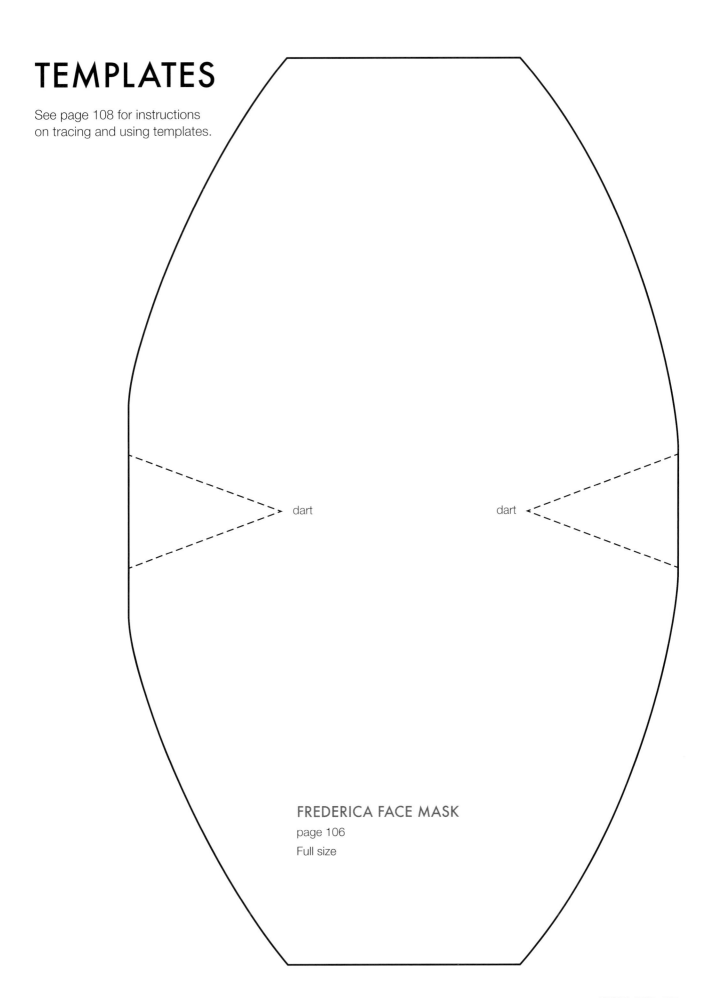

TEMPLATES

See page 108 for instructions
on tracing and using templates.

dart

dart

FREDERICA FACE MASK

page 106

Full size

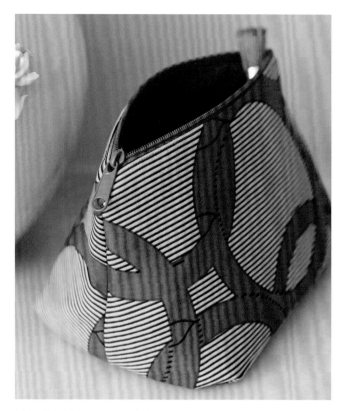

MARILYN MAKE-UP BAG

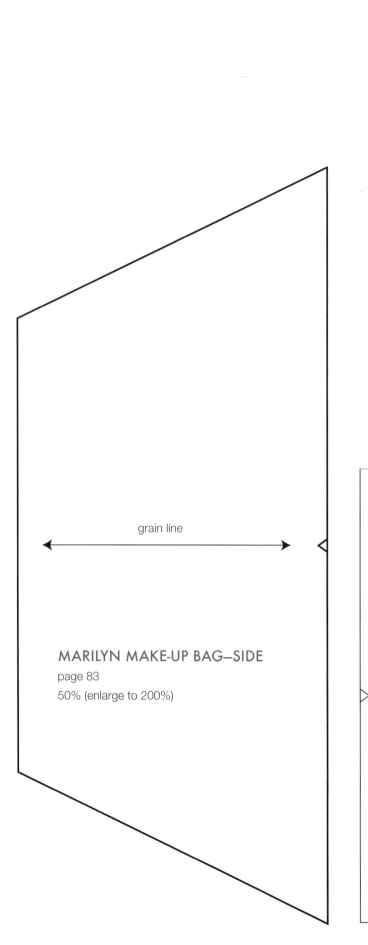

grain line

MARILYN MAKE-UP BAG—SIDE
page 83
50% (enlarge to 200%)

MARILYN MAKE-UP
BAG—BASE
page 83
50% (enlarge to 200%)

place on fold

HARRIET HAIR TIE
page 102
50% (enlarge to 200%)

HARRIET HAIR TIE

EVELYN EYE MASK

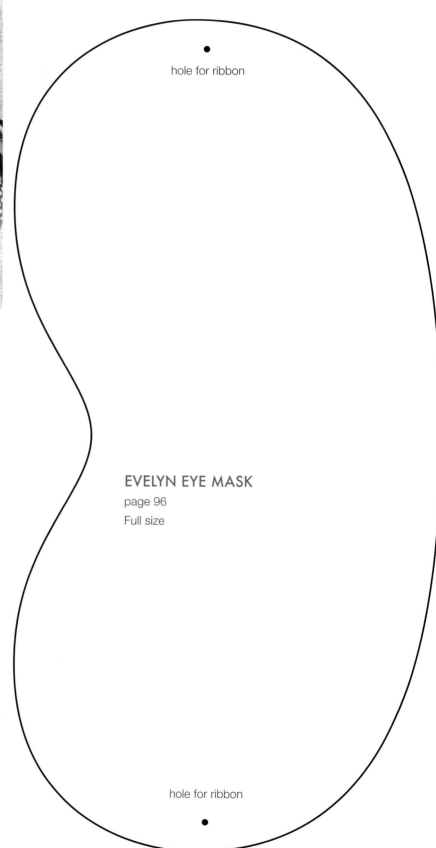

hole for ribbon

EVELYN EYE MASK

page 96

Full size

hole for ribbon

SUPPLIERS AND RESOURCES

AFRICAN WAX PRINT FABRIC RETAILERS

Dovetailed
My own company, for online sales of African wax print fabric by the yard, fat quarters, patterns, sewing supplies, and haberdashery. Orders can be shipped worldwide.
dovetailed.co.uk

VLISCO
Online sales of African wax print fabric
Orders can be shipped worldwide.
vlisco.com

MANUFACTURERS

Vlieseline
Interfacing. Store locator on website.
www.vlieseline.com

UK SEWING AND HABERDASHERY RETAILERS

John Lewis
Haberdashery and sewing supplies
www.johnlewis.com

Hobbycraft
www.hobbycraft.co.uk

William Gee Ltd
London, UK store and online sales.
www.williamgee.co.uk

US SEWING AND HABERDASHERY RETAILERS

Hobby Lobby
www.hobbylobby.com

JoAnn Fabrics and Craft Stores
www.joann.com

Michaels
www.michaels.com

BOOK
Anne Grosfilley, *African Wax Print Textiles* (Prestel, 2018).

WEBSITE
Wax Print Film
waxprintfilm.com

ACKNOWLEDGMENTS

It has been an honour to work on this book and I could not be prouder of this collection of garments and accessories all sewn together in my favorite fabric: African wax print. It is always a joy seeing what the sewing community has been making with these fabrics, and I cannot wait to see all of your creations and pattern "hacks" using this book. Do share your makes using the #dovetailedlondon.

I would like to extend my thanks to Cindy Richards, Penny Craig, Martha Gavin, Anna Galkina, and all the team at CICO Books, and the editor Katie Hardwicke, photographers James Gardiner and Julian Ward, and stylist Nel Haynes. It has been great to work with such a brilliant team!

Finally, to my husband, our three lovely children and to my Mum, words alone cannot express how grateful I am to you all for your continued love and support.

INDEX